COVENANT • BIBLE • STUDIES

Esther

Eugene F. Roop

faithQuest® ✦ Brethren Press®

Cover photo by Vista III Design, Inc.
*The majestic, purple night sky symbolizes Esther, both a queen and a servant of
God's people.*

01 00 99 98 97   5 4 3 2 1

Library of Congress Cataloging-in-Publication Data

Roop, Eugene F., 1942-
      Esther / Eugene F. Roop
          p.   cm. — (Covenant Bible studies)
      ISBN 0-87178-002-X
      1. Bible. O.T. Esther—Study and teaching.   I. Title.
   II. Series: Covenant Bible study series.
   BS1375.5.R66   1997
   222'.9'007—dc20   96-34467

Manufactured in the United States of America

Contents

Foreword

The Covenant Bible Study Series was first developed for a denominational program in the Church of the Brethren and the Christian Church (Disciples of Christ). This program, called People of the Covenant, was founded on the concept of relational Bible study and has been adopted by several other denominations and small groups who want to study the Bible in a community rather than alone.

Relational Bible study is marked by certain characteristics, some of which differ from other types of Bible study. For one, it is intended for small groups of people who can meet face-to-face on a regular basis and share frankly with an intimate group.

It is important to remember that relational Bible study is anchored in covenantal history. God covenanted with people in Old Testament history, established a new covenant in Jesus Christ, and covenants with the church today.

Relational Bible study takes seriously a corporate faith. As each person contributes to study, prayer, and work, the group becomes the real body of Christ. Each one's contribution is needed and important. "For just as the body is one and has many members, and all the members of the body, though many, are one body, so it is with Christ. . . . Now you are the body of Christ and individually members of it" (1 Cor. 12:12,17).

Relational Bible study helps both individuals and the group to claim the promise of the Spirit and the working of the Spirit. As one person testified, "In our commitment to one another and in our sharing, something happened. . . . We were woven together in love by the master Weaver. It is something that can happen only when two or three or seven are gathered in God's name, and we know the promise of God's presence in our lives."

The symbol of these covenant Bible study groups is the burlap cross. The interwoven threads, the uniqueness of each strand, the unrefined fabric, and the rough texture characterize covenant groups. The people in the groups are unique but interrelated; they are imperfect and unpolished, but loving and supportive.

The shape that these divergent threads create is the cross, the symbol for all Christians of the resurrection and presence with us of Christ our Savior. Like the burlap cross, we are brought together, simple and ordinary, to be sent out again in all directions to be in the world.

For people who choose to use this study in a small group, the following guidelines will help create an atmosphere in which support will grow and faith will deepen.

1. As a small group of learners, we gather around God's word to discern its meaning for today.
2. The words, stories, and admonitions we find in scripture come alive for today, challenging and renewing us.
3. All people are learners and all are leaders.
4. Each person will contribute to the study, sharing the meaning found in the scripture and helping to bring meaning to others.
5. We recognize each other's vulnerability as we share out of our own experience, and in sharing we learn to trust others and to be trustworthy.

Additional suggestions for study and group-building are provided in the "Sharing and Prayer" section. They are intended for use in the hour preceding the Bible study to foster intimacy in the covenant group and relate personal sharing to the Bible study topic.

Welcome to this study. As you search the scriptures, may you also search yourself. May God's voice and guidance and the love and encouragement of brothers and sisters in Christ challenge you to live more fully the abundant life God promises.

Preface

Esther is no heroine. Heroines are born to do something great. The rest of us do great things in a pinch, out of necessity. Esther is one of us.

Once in a great while we see real heroes and heroines, people with innate nobleness, brilliance, and character who have saved the day. People like Joan of Arc, Abraham Lincoln, Sojourner Truth, Albert Einstein, and Mahatma Gandhi. I'll never be like them, but I could be like Esther. That's why I like her so much.

Some have been critical of Esther. They think she used feminine wiles instead of the plain truth. They think she was really only saving her own skin, not the lives of all Jews. Some wonder why she downplayed her Jewishness in the beginning, as if she were ashamed of it. And what was all the fuss about her heroic act? Whether she accepted the king's edict or challenged it, she would likely have died. Her decision to fight it was a long shot and not such a tough decision.

That's why Esther is so much like us. We make most of our decisions based on practicality, our own interest or that of our families. We aren't always completely honest and we, too, downplay the parts of our past or our character that will keep us from getting ahead. Anyone who has written a resume knows how to play this game. But when there is a crisis, we can do heroic things, drawing on inner resources we don't use every day.

I don't think most of us were born with these inner resources. I think they are part of our training from an early age. They are the basic rules of living together: Do unto others as you would have them do unto you, help those less fortunate, be kind, be fair, tell the truth, and don't steal. These messages lie under the surface of things and are aroused when we are confronted by injustice or danger. When we need them, we call upon them. But if they are not part of our training, they are not within us to be called upon.

Esther knew the teachings of her faith. For much of her day to day life, she didn't need these teachings, but the day came when she did need them, and they were there. She had no training in human rights work, no political science degree. Her training was in a faith of justice and grace. That was all she needed to respond to the crisis.

We are like that. We don't know the day or the hour that we will need those inner resources of faith, but we hold them in reserve just the same. They are there to help us act in faithful and courageous ways in times that demand it. We also want our children to learn the same values because we want to equip them with resources for crisis and danger. One thing is for sure: they can't use these inner resources if we don't pass the faith story to them.

Esther is much more meaningful to us as an ordinary person who rises to a challenge than as a heroine. She reminds us that the gospel is not a set of ideals that only heroes can attain, but a practical guide that ordinary people, like you and me, take into our very being and live out. Whenever you doubt that faith can make a difference in this world, think of Esther. Think of yourself.

—Julie Garber

Recommended Resources

Anchor Bible Dictionary, Vol. II. "Esther." Doubleday, 1992.

Anderson, Bernhard W. "Esther" (*The Interpreter's Bible*, Vol. III), Abingdon, 1954.

Bergant, Dianne and Robert Karris, eds. *Collegeville Bible Commentary*. Liturgical Press, 1989.

Moore, Carey A., ed. *Esther* (Anchor Bible Series). Doubleday, 1971.

Newsom, Carol A. and Sharon H. Ringe, eds. *Women's Bible Commentary*. Westminster John Knox, 1992.

1

Every Day a Banquet
Esther 1:1-9

Royal banqueting—over a hundred and eighty days of luxurious feasting! Such flamboyant eating and drinking displayed a proud king's wealth. Several days of extravagance set the table for calamity among thousands of his citizens.

Personal Preparation

1. Begin your study by reading the entire story of Esther (even though you may already know the general plot). Reading the whole narrative will refresh your memory with names and details.

2. Learn to pronounce the names of the major characters, so you will not stumble as you read and discuss this story: King Ahasuerus (ah-ha-zu-AY-rus); Mordecai (MOR-duh-ki); Haman (HAY-mun). Try reading aloud the passages containing these names until you have mastered the pronunciations.

3. Take some time to recall mealtimes in your childhood. If you ate potluck dinners at church, what was your favorite covered dish? What is your favorite covered dish now, either to make or to eat?

Understanding

Visualize the church fellowship hall, its long tables covered with paper tablecloths, the countless bowls filled with chicken, baked beans, sliced ham, and taco salad.

The book of Esther is a story for people who like "potlucks." Sometimes it seems that giving a banquet was about all King Ahasuerus could manage. As we shall see, making a decision immobilized him and leadership eluded him. He threw great parties, however. Before we begin to eat, though, let's set the historical scene. In order to grasp the background of Esther, we need to understand two essential elements in this ancient story (and in our stories today): the political context and the cultural milieu.

The Persian Conquest

Nebuchadnezzar of Babylon attacked and destroyed Jerusalem in 587 B.C., forcing many Jewish citizens into exile in the various cities of Babylon. Less than fifty years later, though, the conqueror became the conquered. In 539 B.C. Cyrus of Persia conquered Babylon, transforming the political, social, and religious environment all the way from Egypt to India.

As part of the celebration of his conquest, Cyrus issued an edict: All peoples who had been forcibly resettled by the Babylonians could return to their homeland and revive their religious piety and practice. Some Jews responded to this offer and returned to Palestine, particularly Jerusalem. Many others, however, remained where they had resettled. The Persian takeover changed little in the daily lives of those diaspora Jews (i.e., Jews living dispersed in many countries). They raised their families, ran their businesses, and participated in government on local and national levels.

The cities of Persia in the fourth century B.C., were homes to a diverse population. Most of the time the various ethnic and religious groups lived and worked side by side with minimal tension and strife. But occasionally bad feelings would bubble to the surface and erupt into violence. When such conflicts arose, each of the groups would seek the help of the Persian monarch, claiming the other group as subversive and disloyal. The story of Esther tells about just such a conflict. It was a local, even individual, conflict that, according to the story, swelled into a national emergency.

The problem of ethnic, racial, and religious antagonism has been relived in every age on every continent. Most such conflicts flare at the local level and are resolved without tragedy. Others, however, escalate toward holocaust or fester unresolved for many generations.

It seems that, after centuries of civilization, we still seek to destroy those who are different. And we wonder, How can it keep happening? Diverse people may live and work together for years, yet suddenly an unexpected incident triggers ethnic violence.

The very essence of racial, ethnic, and/or religious identity predisposes one group to interpret the other's differences as deficiencies and distortions. The so-called deficiency may persist for years mostly as an ignored or minor irritant. Nevertheless, passion for a group's own perspective drives the desire to "rectify" the deficiency in the other group. Given almost any excuse, the more dominant community may seek to "correct" the problem, either by coercion or even annihilation. Though the group may describe its goal as peace, righteousness, or justice, the means they employ often lead to death and destruction.

The Banquet Story
Notice that the narrative of Esther opens with a series of three banquets, two given by the king (1:2-4, 5-8) and one by the queen (1:9). To the first banquet the king invited officials ("officials and ministers") and to the second everybody ("both great and small"). The queen invited "the women."

This is a second element for us to understand as background to the story of Esther: the role of the meal. Banquets carry this narrative from beginning to end—showy banquets, celebrative banquets, and dangerous banquets. Indeed, literature from ancient Persia features banquets as central to the life of the Persian royal family.

We are not told the reason for the three banquets or why Queen Vashti gave a separate banquet, so as readers we may be tempted to read a lot into the silence of the narrative. We must be cautious about this, focusing instead on what we do know: banquets play a central role in the story. Not only does the narrative begin and end with banquets given by the king (Esther 8), the story turns at a banquet requested by Esther (Esther 5).

In the chapters to come, we will discuss the banquets in the narrative. For now, let us focus on the importance of the meal in our own lives. Like the ancient peoples, our eating serves more important purposes than nourishment alone.

Consider how much congregations like to eat together, not usually at fancy banquets, but at delicious meals called potluck, covered dish, or "carry-in." Most of us have experienced the importance of mealtime in our family life, too. A great deal of socialization happens at dinner, for instance. Children learn how to participate in conversation, listening as well as speaking, caring for others as well as receiving attention. Children take in not only food, but courtesy, civility, and other expectations of the family.

Adults, as well, have an opportunity to listen and to understand one another and their children around the dinner table. Frequently the most expressive moment of the family's religious piety occurs at mealtime. In many families, dinner constitutes the only family activity that has any consistency and continuity—and usually includes some form of prayer.

In extended families, meals around holidays become the times of re-connection. Parents of adult children frequently invest major time and energy in such meals. Families today rarely live together, work together, or play together, so the family "banquet" becomes the locus of identity, relationship, and expressed love (although sometimes high expectations lead to disappointment and even anger).

The identity of the Christian community also resides in a meal, the Lord's Supper. Grounded in the tradition of Jesus' last supper with his disciples, Christians around the world share this meal with one another as an occasion of spiritual communion. It is the moment when Christians re-enact the Jesus meal and renew their relationship with God and with one another.

The Lord's Supper gives meaning to the many other meals a congregation shares: meals to do business and meals to support projects; meals to celebrate joyful events and meals to remember the loss of loved ones. In many congregations, meals stand alongside worship as the center of community life. At meals the stories of the congregation are told and some conflicts resolved (or irritated). At those blessed banquets, ideas flourish and dreams blossom.

How important are the meals in our fellowship? Well, we know that some members can't recall a single sermon from their childhood.

But they do remember their favorite covered dish.

Discussion and Action

1. Begin by recalling your favorite dishes at potluck dinners when you were a child. Then discuss: Why is eating with other believers important? What does it do for you personally?

2. The banquets referred to in this passage "set the table" for the rest of the story. What, in your opinion, makes for a good meal? How would you describe the role that meals play in your family and congregation? How has the role of the meal changed in your lifetime?

3. Recognizing that we cannot return to an idealized past, what would you like to see happen with meals in family and church?

4. If you have children, what would you say they have learned from mealtime in your family? What have you learned? How could mealtimes become more valuable in your family, as a means of spiritual growth for everyone?

5. We all live in communities with religious and/or ethnic diversity. List some of the aspects of diversity in your community and congregation. Which differences do you consider advantages and which seem to create problems? If the differences were to flare into conflict in your community or congregation, how do you think your group would attempt to resolve the problem?

6. Think now beyond your community. The European holocaust represents the most horrendous tragedy in the twentieth century, when a religious/ethnic difference was seen as a deficiency and the "deficient" Jews destroyed. But there have been, and are, others. List occasions in history or events in the present when ethnic, social, and religious differences have flared into trouble. Take time to remember and to pray about those situations.

7. As time permits explore issues, questions, and insights that you have not touched upon in your discussion time. From your reading through the book of Esther,

what issues or questions were raised for you? What new insights did you receive from your reading, and what do you hope to learn in this study during the coming weeks?

2

Incompetent Leadership
Esther 1:10-22

When the king orders a public display of beauty by his wife, Vashti, the queen refuses. What should be done? According to the lawyers, the insolent act must be punished, lest this time-honored principle fall into disrepute—that "every man should be master in his own house."

Personal Preparation

1. Review Esther 1:1-9 and carefully read 1:10-22. Recall the kinds of leadership you have experienced over the years. What qualities in a leader have encouraged you to be a willing follower?
2. Look also at Proverbs 31:10ff. This portrayal of the "obedient" wife may provide a backdrop for the tension in the story. In your opinion, what is the role of obedience in Christian marriage relationships today?
3. Obedience to authority will provide one focus for our attention. Recall a situation in which you felt your own disobedience was justified. On what facts or principles did you base your justification?

Understanding

Writer Laurence J. Peter quipped: "If at first you don't succeed, you may be at your level of incompetence already." This rewording of the classic maxim seems appropriate when we relate it to the leadership blunders of King Ahasuerus. His incompetence shows through in our narrative today, as he waits until he is "merry with wine" to issue a dubious command. Though a seemingly small request, it gave rise to rash declarations on a grand scale.

Queen Vashti Refused to Come

The narrative says little about the banquet events except that the end of the seven-day party found King Ahasuerus under the influence of alcohol. In that condition, he ordered Queen Vashti brought before him "to show the peoples and the officials her beauty." According to the text, the queen was to be "wearing the royal crown" (v. 11). That phrase has prompted endless speculation by readers. Conjecture about the queen's attire has ranged from royal elegance to . . . nothing but a crown! Of one thing we can be certain: the narrative is clear about the *reason* for the command appearance. The king wanted to show off his wife's beauty.

Queen Vashti refused to come. We don't know why. The queen's separate banquet listed in the opening verses (1:9) may suggest that this clash had a history. The reticence of the narrative to say more has long stirred the imagination of readers. In some traditions, Vashti's disobedience has been attributed to her wickedness. Others have portrayed her as heroic for refusing to be "used" by the king. Whatever the cause, her refusal enraged her husband.

Proverbs 31 describes the ideal wife as one who "does good" for her husband and "not harm" (31:12). The order of family life reflected in several New Testament texts similarly reinforces a structure that defines the wife's relationship to the husband in terms of obedience (see Eph. 5:22). Interpreters differ about how we are to understand these texts. Today, by taking clues from other parts of the New Testament, particularly the way Jesus dealt with people, the church has moved to an understanding of marriage characterized by mutuality more than subordination.

The story of Esther relates to a time in which most relationships, including marriage, operated according to a strict hierarchy of obedience. Nevertheless, even in relationships based on command and obedience (between monarch and subject, for example), the Bible recognizes limits to obedience. For example, one does not obey a command to do evil, to worship other divine beings. The stories of Daniel, portraying the same era as the Esther narrative, boldly address such limits to obedience.

Even if we concede that blind obedience is inappropriate, we constantly face two issues as tough decisions come our way: (1) knowing whether we have the right reasons for deciding to disobey and (2) being willing to accept the consequences of disobedience. When must we disobey civil, religious, or even family authority? Wisdom has taught us to test any decision of conscience with the Bible and with the community of faith.

Yet very often the decision to disobey is a very lonely moment. John Kline (1797-1864) prospered as a Virginia farmer, teacher, and physician. Like most members of the Church of the Brethren, Kline opposed both slavery and war. When war did come to the states, John Kline vigorously argued for military exemption for Brethren and others who opposed war because of their faith.

John Kline traveled with the support of his church and firm biblical convictions opposing violence and military service. Nevertheless, this man of commitment and integrity was openly distrusted because of his willingness to render medical aid to victims on both sides of the civil conflict. Finally that distrust burst into the violence he opposed. John Kline was ambushed and assassinated while traveling alone on June 15, 1864.

John Kline tested his decision with the community and the Bible. Even with all this support to live a different way, his final moment may have been one like that of Jesus in the garden: "Remove this cup from me" (Mark 14:36).

You can no doubt think of instances in your own life, maybe far less dramatic, when the issue of obedience was every bit as complicated and difficult. And the consequences may also have been, in some crucial way, life-giving or life-deadening. At times like these, how do you decide?

For whatever reason, Queen Vashti decided to disobey; she lost her crown and disappeared from the story. Tradition has speculated that she was executed. Anticipating the high cost of disobedience has coerced many to obey, even against their better judgment. It has always been easier to talk about the criteria for justifiable disobedience in the abstract than to deal with it in a particular circumstance.

Nor should we romanticize those who disobey according to their conscience. The history of the church reveals that decisions attributed to conscience have resulted in disaster. Religious wars have been fought and "infidels" annihilated on the basis of conscience. Conscience can be used to justify destructive decisions as often as it is used to explain heroic actions.

A National Disgrace

The king, angry, but apparently unsure of what to do, consulted his advisors (1:13ff.). As we shall see throughout this narrative, King Ahasuerus seldom decides a matter for himself, choosing instead to take the recommendations of his advisors. In the matter of Queen Vashti's disobedience, the advisors were clear. This domestic dispute threatened to embolden women throughout Persia to disobey their husbands: "There will be no end of contempt and wrath" by the wives of the empire (1:18). The advisors concluded that this single act by the queen would destroy the social fabric of the empire! (The narrative expects us to laugh, or at least shake our heads, at this inane counsel.) The solution of the advisors was to depose the queen! This advice pleased the king.

The fear expressed by these royal advisors seems oddly familiar. They concluded that the social fabric of the Persian empire was so fragile that one misstep by a high-profile person would cause society to disintegrate. Apparently, we are not the first to worry that society and the family are about to fall apart.

We all recognize the importance of a vibrant, solid, social environment. The health of the social climate affects all of our relationships. No social environment can be both stagnant and vibrant. Change must happen. In every age some changes in the social milieu will lead toward a more just and healthy world, while other innovations will threaten destruction. It takes wise discernment and listening prayer to know the difference. In reviewing history we find that even faithful disciples will disagree. Most problematic are those folk who, like the king's advisors, dramatically overreact to any perceived threat. They almost always end up on the wrong side of God's future.

Difficult Decisions

Our biblical narrative opens with a focus on leadership, particularly on how leadership can go wrong. This command-

and-refusal incident raises difficult issues, even while portraying the king as inept and the advisors as incompetent.

We expect our leaders to lead, but no one person is wise enough to see all the options or understand all the nuances within a complicated situation. Therefore, we want them to consult before acting. Leadership requires the faithful, earnest advice of colleagues and those who have traveled the path of experience. Advisors can be incompetent, however, and, as we shall see later in this story, they can be corrupt. Consultation does not relieve the leader of the responsibility to decide wisely. Leadership in some eras has seemed especially difficult, and many folks in our culture today have concluded that all leaders are either corrupt or incompetent, making leadership quite difficult and good leadership hard to identify.

Perhaps you have heard the often repeated story of the sandhill crane. It seems these large birds fly for miles, across vast stretches of our continent, displaying some of the patterns that many consider important to good leadership. The birds apparently rotate leadership, for no single bird is always out in front. They appear to choose leaders that can handle the turbulent air that comes with being out in front, where there is no windbreak. Finally, as one bird leads, the rest follow close behind, constantly honking out encouragement.

Though we need wise and dedicated leaders who know how to make decisions, we also need followers dedicated to encouraging appropriately those who bear the burden of responsibility. Any form of leadership can be a lonely task, and our leaders need words of blessing from those who follow. Sometimes, of course, the noise we make seems to be overwhelming. At other times our words revive the strength and renew the spirit of our leaders.

Discussion and Action

1. Share about the kinds of leadership you have experienced, and discuss the admirable qualities you've observed in good leaders. Make a two-column list of good and bad leadership characteristics. Then discuss: Who are the good leaders today in politics, the community, your church? Are these good leaders in troubling positions?

2. Based on your readings of Proverbs 31:10ff, talk about the role of obedience in Christian marriage relationships today. Does the word *obedience* have other than negative connotations for marriage? Should obedience be limited to one gender?

3. Focus on Queen Vashti's response to the king's request. Explore some actual situations where obedience was required and a person responded with disobedience. Recall the author's statement: "It has always been easier to talk about the criteria for justifiable disobedience in the abstract than to deal with it in a particular circumstance."

4. What changes in social patterns do you find most healthy? What changes do you fear will be most destructive? Discuss the royal advisors' apparent overreaction to the queen's disobedience. What does "dramatically overreacting" look like in our society today? Can you point to some specific examples?

5. Although we live in a more egalitarian society than the one reflected in the narrative, we still face difficult decisions regarding obedience as citizens, employees, and family and church members. Name some criteria you use when making decisions about obedience to an authority.

6. Leadership involves a complex process of listening and deciding. It is often easy to identify those in leadership who listen too long and decide too little, or who listen too little and decide too quickly. Describe leaders who have discovered the balance between listening and acting. When have you been either the leader or the advisor to a leader when the balance has seemed right?

7. Brainstorm some ways of actively encouraging leaders in your church and community. For example, how often do your pastor and/or elders hear about what is *right* in the church?

3

A Queen with Charisma
Esther 2:1-23

Recalling the put-down by his wife, Ahasuerus took the advice of his attendants. He tried to make Vashti an example to all the women of the realm. As a result, a new queen had to be found, a woman with youth, beauty, and character. Enter Esther—a woman with charisma.

Personal Preparation

1. Reread Esther 1, continuing on through chapter 2. You may find the second chapter a little difficult to follow. If so, make some notes about the specific points where the narrative veers away from the main thread of the story to include other information and anecdotes.
2. *Difference* is a key word in this chapter. Jot down some other words and images that come to mind when you consider this word. When you have been different from a group in any way, has it been a positive experience for you?
3. Name people, the famous and not so famous, who you feel have charismatic qualities? Before reading further, write down the name of a woman with charisma. What gives her that special character?

Understanding

Perhaps you have heard the apocryphal story of Miss Jones, a lonely lady, who was for many years the oldest resident of a small midwestern town. When she died, the editor of the local newspaper wanted to print a caption commemorating her death. But as he thought about it, he realized that, while Miss Jones had never done anything terribly wrong in her life, she had never actually done anything noteworthy either.

As this editor walked to his office to write the obituary, he ran into the owner of the tombstone establishment in the little community. This man, too, wondered what to say about Miss Jones. The editor decided to assign the first reporter he met the task of writing up a short statement suitable for both the paper and the tombstone. Upon returning to the office, he found only the sports editor at his desk.

So . . . they say if you pass through that small town, you will find a tombstone reading like this:

> Here lie the bones of Nancy Jones.
> For her, life held no terrors.
> She lived alone.
> She died at home.
> No hits, no runs, no errors.

What a picture of the plague of mediocrity! Certainly the motto—To avoid criticism, do nothing—was not the way of Esther. Ahasuerus may have thought he was getting a show-piece, but we'll see her stepping into the most risky situations, becoming noteworthy for her charismatic leadership.

Choosing a Queen

The narrative introduction, Esther 1:1—3:7, lays out for us the events that led to Esther's coronation as queen. After explaining why Vashti lost the job (1:10-22), the narrative turns to the process leading to Esther's appointment.

As before, King Ahasuerus consulted his advisors regarding the search process for a new queen. They recommended that qualified candidates be gathered from all provinces of the realm. They identified three qualifications for the new queen: appearance (beautiful), age (young), and sexual experience (none). The young candidates were to be placed in the care of the royal official Hegai, who would provide for the best presentation of each woman to the king. The king would then make the selection. Predictably, the king accepted the counsel of his advisors (2:4).

Unpredictably, Hegai found himself especially taken by Esther, a young woman from Susa. He gave Esther extra attention, giving her the best chance of being selected. Each young woman, given whatever she wanted for the "interview," went before the king in the evening and returned the next morning. When it was Esther's turn, she took with her only what her palace patron, Hegai, recommended. It worked, for "the king loved Esther more than all the other women; . . . she won his favor and devotion" (2:17). Esther was chosen.

Does the lack of description of the actual "interview" spark your imagination, as it has for many other readers? Such descriptive reticence is common in biblical narratives. You and I have the opportunity to replay that part of the story as we wish, while the biblical focus rests on other matters: Esther's character and qualifications. We may assume that she met the qualifications; however, that was apparently not the deciding factor in her selection.

Our narrator repeatedly describes Esther as a woman who stood out from the others, "admired by all who saw her." There must have been something different about this woman, an intangible element that set her apart from the other beautiful, young virgins. Hegai, who presumably had no sexual interest in Esther, noticed this "difference," as did the king. We are not told what made Esther different—just that everyone noticed. Because of it she won Hegai's favor, the king's devotion, and the admiration of all who saw her.

What is it about a person that elicits such a response? Apparently it is not simply a matter of age or beauty. We frequently call it *charisma*, a Greek word that means "specially graced." Much of our advertising uses one form of charisma to sell products. Charisma also affects our political process, frequently functioning as the primary criterion for electability. Often in the public realm, charisma depends heavily on beauty and/or another valued quality. But we know that divinely inspired charisma, being specially gifted by God, goes beyond beauty and charm. The Bible often uses other words to describe this charisma, like the Hebrew *kavod* or the Greek *doxa*. The Hebrew word connotes weight and presence, describing one worthy of "glory" (Job 19:9). *Doxa* suggests light and splendor, one who radiates "glory" (Luke 12:27). Where do you find such charisma?

Life as a Minority

Our narrator steps aside from this main thread of the story to provide other information about Esther. She was a Jewish orphan, adopted by her cousin Mordecai (2:7). Twice the narrator tells us that Mordecai advised Esther not to reveal her ethnic/religious identity while she was a candidate for queen (2:10, 20). Esther took her guardian's advice.

The Jews lived in the Persian cities as a minority. Although the first Persian king, Cyrus, had granted them the right to return to Jerusalem, in the two generations since their grandparents' deportation, the Jews had established homes and developed work. Thus, most Jews continued to live in the multi-ethnic cities of Persia. We know that several cities in the Persian (and later Greek) empire had vigorous Jewish communities.

The story of Esther reminds us that it is seldom an advantage to be in the minority. Life as a minority can be difficult in the best of times. Everyday life keeps minorities aware of their "differentness." For example, have you noticed that the religious calendar of a majority group generally functions as the calendar of business and education as well? The values of the majority frequently become law. The friendships within the majority community often override ability as a factor in success. Minorities report having to grit their teeth as they try to ignore words that belittle them and stories that portray them as "losers."

Occasionally the status of a minority person or group can quickly change from acceptance (at least toleration) to being "the enemy." There is seldom a single cause for such a terrible turn. A seemingly unrelated event can trigger a long-simmering feud or resentment, as has happened in the Balkan states and some African states. The majority, sensing a threat to their culture, might seek to purge and purify rather than change and accommodate. That, in fact, occurred in Nazi Germany, Stalinist Russia, and Shiite Iran. The Jews have a well-documented history of such victimization, stretching across the centuries and around the globe.

Actually, our own Euro-American community in North America has a long history of dealing with racial, ethnic, and religious minorities. On the one hand, that history tells of acceptance, accommodation, and incorporation. But the story also includes the deportation of the native population, the enslavement of the African population, and the internment of Asians. Even in the best of times, minorities struggle against great odds in North America. Hopefully, we will extend the hand of fellowship as we seek to grow in hospitality toward people who are different.

The Conspiracy

The narrator now offers one additional, seemingly peripheral, bit of information. Mordecai learned of a plot to assassinate the king (2:21-23). Two of the palace guards were angry with the king (we can only speculate about the reason), which turned into a deadly anger for these conspirators. Mordecai told Queen Esther of the conspiracy, and she relayed the information to the king. The conspirators were executed, and the threat to the throne was averted.

This anecdote comes at the end of the chapter without explanation or integration. It will matter later on, but for now these verses simply tell us the royal household of Persia, like government today, experienced political schemes arising out of the desire for power. The incident also signals that in matters of palace intrigue, Esther and Mordecai will be found on the side of the king—a fact Ahasuerus will only belatedly remember.

Discussion and Action

1. Refer to Personal Preparation, number three, and tell about people you have named—particularly women—who have charisma. What gives these people their special qualities?

2. List some ways individuals are appointed to positions of power and leadership. Here the king's advisors set up a process whereby all the candidates who meet the criteria are gathered for an interview with the king, who makes the final selection. Whether in the church or in business and industry, selection processes are frequently a matter of debate, with everyone wanting a hand in the selection process. Discuss the values that should be reflected in such processes.

3. Recall and list some of the tragedies that have resulted from majority/minority conflict—past and present,

international and local. What can we do to help prevent such catastrophes?

4. Some futurists expect to see a society (and church) formed like a quilt, with homogeneous communities being loosely held together by certain common threads. Others envision a society in which groupings based on race, ethnicity, and other differences mostly disappear, the whole being more tightly woven. Which kind of future do you expect? Which kind of future would you prefer? What biblical perspectives help inform your preference?

5. In past years the Miss America contest has flirted with the idea of eliminating the swimsuit competition. But viewers have insisted it be retained. In your opinion, what is true beauty? In what ways are you influenced by outward appearance? Does physical beauty have any positive role?

6. In your community or congregation, who are the majority and minority people? What feelings arise as a result of being a minority? How does the permanent minority deal with those feelings? How are—or should—the minority voices be heard?

7. Those living with the AIDS virus make up a minority group in society today. Your group could take action by cutting out quilt blocks for a baby with AIDS. Or you could consider calling a local group that works with AIDS patients to get their ideas for a practical service project.

4

Injustice Intended
Esther 3:1-15

When he appointed Haman to high political office, the king may not have realized the volatility of his new official's temperament. On the basis of a perceived slight—Mordecai's refusal to bow to him—Haman hatched a plan to destroy an entire people. Though such overreactions shock us, they continue to occur, even today. One must beware the temptation to let pride and power prompt evil plans and revenge.

Personal Preparation

1. Review Esther 1 and 2. Then read 3:1-15 from the perspective of each of the characters in the story. What, in your opinion, are some of their inner motivations?
2. We use the word *injustice* frequently. Write down your definition of that word. What biblical stories would you use to illustrate injustice? How would the third chapter of Esther rate in this regard?
3. If you had to name at least three "high points of tension and conflict" in Esther 1—3, what sections would you choose?

Understanding

The *Minneapolis Tribune* once gave a report about a federal judge in Texas who instructed a jury to return a verdict of innocent in a car-theft case. When the jury filed back into the courtroom after a very brief discussion, the foreman dutifully announced: "We find the boy that stole the car not guilty, your honor."

No one needs to remind us that occasionally injustice can overwhelm justice in many of our courtrooms. On a personal level, virtually all of us can name occasions when we have suffered an injustice or betrayal. Some of those experiences may have been devastating, perhaps even criminal. Or perhaps they seemed more serious at the time than they do in retrospect. At any rate, you and I—like Mordecai of ancient days—are familiar with the seething antagonism of people looking to take unfair advantage and destroy others.

Ancient Antagonism
As the extended introduction draws to a close (3:1-6), we meet Haman, the villain in our biblical melodrama. We are given only one item of information about him: he was an Agagite. Nevertheless, that seemingly incidental fragment of data connects the story's tension to an ancient antagonism. In 1 Samuel 15 we are told about King Agag of the Amalekites, whom Saul defeated but spared from execution. Exodus 17 describes the Amalekite attack on the Israelites as they journeyed from Egypt to the promised land. Genesis 36 identifies Amalek as the grandson of Esau.

This small bit of information about Haman pulls into the story a long memory of bitter antagonism between Israel and one of its neighbors living on the east side of the Jordan River. Apparently the simmering feud between Israel and Amalek was to emerge again in the story of Esther. History shows that memories of injustice and violation can affect relationships many generations into the future.

The Decalogue declares that God remembers human unfaithfulness only to the third and fourth generation of those who reject God (Exod. 20:5). Yet families often hold grudges about perceived injustices and betrayals much longer than that! In some African communities, elders continue to retell stories of violations and injuries suffered at the hands of other tribal groups centuries before. Such memories fuel a bitterness that can break into inter-tribal wars.

Of course, long-standing victim stories are not limited to traditional tribal groups. Events in a church congregation can cause one family or group to feel mistreated or betrayed. Sometimes the "victim story" persists because the perceived offense was never adequately explored and resolved. Even if a congregation endeavors to handle such a dispute fairly, however, that does not ensure the antagonists will lay it to rest. Hurt feelings and animosity will continue to threaten the future as long as the stories are retold without ending in forgiveness and/or reconciliation.

In spite of all our efforts, justice remains difficult to define and even harder to incorporate into our interpersonal relationships. Poetry often seems more adequate than prose to describe justice. Anglican clergyman Sydney Smith over a century ago observed in verse: "Truth is justice's handmaid, freedom is its child, peace is its companion, safety walks in its steps, victory follows in its train; it is the brightest emanation from the gospel; it is the attribute of God."

Royal Promotion

Revenge, not justice, was Haman's intention. Esther 3 reports that Haman was promoted to the position of chief royal advisor. We are not told the reason for this promotion, but it follows immediately after the anecdote in which Mordecai helps the king by reporting an assassination plot. Common wisdom suggests that Mordecai would have received some reward for his loyalty, perhaps a promotion. Instead, the promotion went to Haman.

The king commanded that all the other royal advisors should bow down to Haman. In doing so they would signal their recognition of Haman's primacy. But Mordecai refused to bow down. Though the narrator does not tell us the reason for his refusal, tradition has provided many different explanations. Ancient Jewish writings offer reasons related to Mordecai's character and his abhorrence of religious idolatry. The Greek edition of Esther suggests that Mordecai refused because one should only bow down to God. Other biblical figures, however, including Abraham, Jacob and David, bow to people out of politeness or subservience (see Gen. 18:2; 33:3; 1 Sam. 24:8).

Mordecai himself refused to explain his action and, predictably, his public slight infuriated Haman. Haman chose not to exact revenge at that moment, but upon learning that Mordecai was a Jew, he decided to destroy not only the offender, but all of his people as well!

Power and position within any organization carry with

them the potential for conflict, as illustrated by the situation between Haman and Mordecai. Sometimes such tension cannot be avoided, regardless of how the positions are assigned and the power distributed. Arguments over position and power arose among the disciples of Jesus and constantly afflicted the earliest churches. We should not expect our congregations today to be exempt from such disputes.

The task for the congregation, institution, or organization is to handle conflicts wisely. This requires groups to forthrightly define roles and responsibilities fairly and clearly. Unfortunately, when organizational matters generate enormous anger, it often seems easier to assess blame than to find ways to move forward.

Haman's Evil Plans
The story now begins with Haman's evil plan to destroy Mordecai and his people (3:8ff.). Haman told King Ahasuerus about a group in the empire whose presence and practices were threatening royal law and order and that he should not tolerate such a group. Haman recommended that the king completely wipe it out and added that he would personally fund the royal treasury if the king accepted his recommendation. The king's acceptance was never in doubt. After all, Haman was the chief advisor to a king with a history of automatically accepting the advice of his counselors.

Ahasuerus delegated to Haman and his secretaries the responsibility of drafting the decree that would destroy the dangerous minority. In addition, the king gave Haman the right to sign the decree in the royal name. The narrative does not indicate that the king had been informed about the reason for Haman's plan, or even the identity of the dangerous minority. The king simply delegated the responsibility to his "trusted" advisor.

In the first month of the year, Haman drafted a decree that ordered annihilation of all the Jews, regardless of age, gender, or location. The royal courier hurried to distribute the decree and prepare for its execution. The holocaust was to be carried out in the twelfth month, allowing a little time but not much hope.

At the close of the twentieth century, we cannot shrug off genocide as an ancient problem of unenlightened and un-

Christian people. Holocaust in our century destroyed whole Jewish communities in Europe. Even in North America, only a few raised their voices in serious objection or wept publicly. We lift up as heroic those who helped to rescue Jews from the Nazi decree of annihilation, yet there were all too few heros. In U.S. history, holocaust nearly destroyed the Native American population. Not until two hundred years later have we begun to acknowledge that tragedy. No people and no century can claim to be guilt free.

What about us? Have we committed transgressions of justice and fairness within our relationships? How have we used power or authority in destructive ways? For any of us, it's never too late to choose a new path, to take the first small step toward reconciliation and, if need be, restitution.

The story is told that one day the nineteenth-century Swedish chemist Alfred Nobel sat down to read his morning paper and was horrified to find his own obituary staring him in the face: "Alfred Nobel, inventor of dynamite, died yesterday. He had devised a method for killing more people in a war than ever before. He died a rich man."

Actually, Alfred's older brother was the one who had died; a newspaper reporter had the name wrong. The mistaken obituary, however, weighed heavily on Nobel's mind for days. He concluded that he wanted to be remembered for something more worthy than a better method of human destruction— and the fortune that he had accumulated from it! So he initiated the Nobel Prize, the award for scientists and writers who work for peace in the world. Nobel said, "Every[one] ought to have the chance to correct his epitaph in midstream and write a new one."

In Esther, an evil decree rang out in the land because of an evil advisor and an incompetent king. There are always reasons; there can be no excuse. Hope rests in acknowledging our past, while our lives are still unfolding. Few things will change us as much as a sober look at the heritage we will leave at our life's end.

Discussion and Action

1. Share your definitions of injustice from your personal preparation. What biblical stories did you find to illustrate injustice?

2. From Personal Preparation, number three, what high points of tension and conflict did you name? Why?

3. Consider the nature of grudges: personal and institutional. Name grudges you've felt were held against you, or that you held against others. How do the political "games people play" in office and school politics contribute to ongoing feuds?

4. What role do memories of injustice play in your life? Have the stories been resolved through either reconciliation or forgiveness? Have you been able to lay them to rest, or do they still come back, complete with intense feelings?

5. Congregations as well as individuals have memories of injustice. Do some congregational stories remain almost too painful to retell? Do some people still refuse to lay an incident to rest? Are you or someone you know one of those people? What is required for healing to take place?

6. Ahasuerus apparently delegated responsibility to Haman without giving the necessary supervision. Yet no one wants a supervisor constantly "looking over the shoulder" or undercutting decisions. What are the marks of good oversight and supervision? When is it too intense? insufficient?

7. Share your response to the author's statement: "Unfortunately, when organizational matters generate enormous anger, it often seems easier to assess blame than to find ways to move forward." When have you seen this principle in action? What happened? What is your advice in such situations?

8. Discuss some of the holocaust tragedies in our time or culture. You might view a movie or videotaped documentary to energize the discussion. How can we get past feeling uninvolved ("It was not me or my fault") without being preoccupied by guilt?

5

A Defining Moment
Esther 4:1-17

Informed of Haman's evil plot, Esther had to make a decision. Knowing that approaching the king without permission could mean her death, she faced paying the ultimate price for the sake of others. It would be a defining moment for her and for her people.

Personal Preparation

1. Review Haman's plan in Esther 3:7-15. Then carefully read Esther 4:1-17. In what ways does Mordecai's plan oppose Haman's in this narrative? In your opinion, was it a wise plan?
2. Have you experienced what you would call a "defining moment"? Think through the circumstances. To what extent was God's presence and/or guidance evident to you at the time?
3. Most readers know that God is not explicitly named in the narrative of Esther. Yet most sense God's hidden presence at key points in this story. Have there been occasions in your life when you could not "see" God at the time but later recognized that God was present?

Understanding

Perhaps you have seen the colorful wall poster displaying a field of wildflowers with snow-covered mountain peaks in the background. The caption underneath says: "Do not follow where the path may lead. Follow God, instead, where there is no path . . . and leave a trail."

Often, in the heat of the moment, we see no clear path to decision. It has often been only in hindsight that I could detect God's presence and guidance in making personal decisions.

In the events narrated in 3:1-17, Esther especially could see no clear path. She had to hew out a path filled with risky decisions in the face of life-threatening uncertainty.

Mordecai's Response

Upon hearing about the decree of destruction, Mordecai engaged in a ritual of distress. In ancient Israel, the ritual of sackcloth and ashes played an important role in several circumstances of distress. It functioned for Jacob (Gen. 37:34) and David (2 Sam. 3:31) as a ritual of mourning. Israel's King Ahab engaged in the ritual as an act of repentance (1 Kgs. 19). Mordecai combined sackcloth and ashes with a "bitter cry," the cry of the oppressed (Exod. 3:7). Mordecai was not alone in this distress. As news spread, the Jewish community throughout the empire expressed its response through this traditional ritual.

Esther received the bad news, too. We do not know exactly what she was told. Esther responded not to the decree, but to Mordecai's distress. The fact that Mordecai subsequently sent Esther a copy of the decree suggests that she didn't originally know the cause of Mordecai's anguish. Therefore, she may not have understood why Mordecai engaged in the ritual of distress. Nevertheless, this occasioned the first interaction between Esther and Mordecai in the story.

Mordecai and Esther

This interaction between Esther and Mordecai began through a messenger, Hathach. Gradually, as the intensity of their exchange increased, Hathach's participation gradually decreased until Mordecai and Esther seemed to be talking directly to one another (see Esther 4:15). Yet we are not told that they actually met.

This narrative movement seems to mirror many of our own conversations. First, we maintain a polite distance. Gradually, the engagement becomes more intense, through familiarity or even anger, and the distance disappears, either emotionally or physically. In this story Esther begins by sending clothes to

Mordecai, encouraging him to end his ritual of distress. He did not accept them. Then Esther sent Hathach to investigate the problem. Mordecai not only told Hathach about the decree of destruction, but Mordecai revealed his plan to reverse the decree. He wanted Esther to go to the king "to make supplication to him and entreat him for her people" (4:8).

Esther sent word back, explaining why Mordecai's plan would not work. Anyone going to the king, except by invitation, would be executed. Everybody in the whole realm knew that! Furthermore, Esther had not been invited into the king's presence for a month (4:11).

The level of the conversation intensified dramatically. Mordecai sent back word that Esther had better not assume that she would escape the death plot. Also if she refused to help, deliverance would come from elsewhere, while Esther and her household would perish. Whether she helped or whether she didn't, Esther could die! Backing off from this threat, Mordecai added, "Who knows? Perhaps you have come to royal dignity for just such a time as this" (4:14).

The Critical Moment

Mordecai articulated the belief that key moments arise in the human drama. At such moments individuals can make a critical difference. We often tell history as the story of such "defining moments." Each nation, race, and community knows the story of women and men whose impact changed history. Individuals frequently tell their own stories of people who, by word or deed, made a difference at an important moment in their lives. Sometimes the critical moment is public and/or obvious, as in the story of Esther. At other times we see the moment only as we look back.

Mordecai suggested that person, position, and circumstance must all come together in order to change the course of events. Esther found herself in the "right" position at the critical time. It was now her decision. She replied directly to Mordecai, instructing him to gather the Jewish community of Susa for a three-day fast. Following that ritual fast, Esther would go to the king, even in direct violation of royal law. In grim determination, she said it all: "If I perish, I perish" (4:16).

Esther counted the cost, for she could die. The opportunity to change history seldom comes without risk to the one called upon to act. Yet why are we often surprised by the riskiness of the call to conform our lives individually and corporately into the image of Jesus (see Rom. 8:29)? The process involves the promise of peace, but it is rarely a gentle, easy, or "safe" venture and can be quite lonely. Here's how Alan Jones describes action in his book *Soul Making:*

> Yes, love has teeth! It asks us one terrible and demanding question: "What are you going to *do* now? Now that you've stopped blaming your mother, your husband, your wife, your environment, the communists, the capitalists, the atheists, the fundamentalists . . . What are you going to do?" Being a lover, becoming a soul, means making choices.

Esther made the lonely decision for risky action. And with this decision, she took control of the narrative action. Others responded to her initiatives. Previously, she had been fairly passive; having been gathered up in the search for a queen, she did as she was told in that process. Then Esther began to initiate the actions in the story. She gave direct instructions to Mordecai, who "did everything as Esther had ordered him" (4:17). The narrative power shifted from the men in the story to the woman.

An Unnamed Presence
Our story of Esther, as found in the Hebrew Bible, does not present God as a named actor in the drama. Perhaps we would prefer to see Esther and Mordecai praying, and then God acting. However, God remains in the background, discerned only by the eyes of faith. This manner of narration gives the reader the responsibility to perceive God's presence. Some readers have seen a reference to God in Mordecai's statement that "relief and deliverance will rise for the Jews from another quarter" (4:14). And others have suggested that prayer was a part of the fasting ritual directed by Esther (4:16). In neither case, though, does the narrative require such conclusions.

A biblical narrative with God being visible only to the eyes of faith; a book of the Bible that doesn't use the word *God*—Is that a gift or a problem? God's presence does not depend on our recognition or acknowledgment. Catholic theologian Karl

Rahner writes, "I know that this word '[God]' is obscure, by definition the most obscure word there can be, the word which is genuinely impossible to include among other words of human language as one more word. But I know that what is meant by the word may be present in a person's life, even if its name is never spoken by the person."

Each of us has been entrusted with the responsibility to discern God's presence in our own lives. We cannot expect that God will announce the divine presence in neon lights or on the information super highway. In the biblical narratives of Esther and Ruth, we have the opportunity to discern with eyes of faith the unseen presence of God, a task that remains our responsibility in our lifelong journey of faith.

And we are called to act, as Esther did, usually without being sure of our motives or in any way confident of the outcome. In the *Magnificent Defeat,* writer Frederick Buechner masterfully frames this challenge we face:

> The voice that we hear over our shoulders never says, "First be sure that your motives are pure and selfless and then follow Me." If it did, then we could none of us follow. So when later the voice says, "Take up your cross and follow Me," at least part of what is meant by "cross" is our realization that we are seldom any less than nine parts fake. Yet our feet can insist on answering Him anyway. And on we go, step after step, mile after mile. How far? How far?

Discussion and Action

1. From Personal Preparation, number two, share about the events you would name as "defining moments" in your life. What people played an important role? What aspects of the situation required risky decision-making and action? To what extent was God's presence and guidance evident to you?

2. Respond to the caption on the wall poster described at the beginning of this lesson. Explain why you agree or disagree with it. Have you pondered an important decision and not seen with clarity the path ahead?

3. We seldom pay attention to the dynamics of conversation, including the elements of position and touch.

When have you seen people move closer together—or farther apart—as their conversation became more intense and animated?

4. Intense emotion causes some people to step forward and others to step back. What does it mean to give a person "space" in conversation? Does a faith commitment affect how we physically react in talking with one another?

5. We celebrate people who have acted to turn national, religious, or personal history in a positive direction. Recall and discuss critical moments in national, religious, and family history. Who responded to the challenges of such times?

6. In some critical moments, it seems that no one steps forward to help. Or the most influential figure acts to destroy rather than to enhance life. When have you seen this happen? What things can Christians do to help prevent this kind of inaction?

7. A distress ritual, combined with the lament Psalms (see, for example, Psalms 13 and 22) afforded our biblical ancestors an accepted means to express the overwhelming feelings that accompany death, illness, sin, and catastrophe. Most communities have continued to employ similar rituals, though the European-American Christian community has not developed a ritual of distress. What are some of the effects of this?

6

Approaching Authority
Esther 5:1-14

Esther determined to make a life or death approach to the king. Exactly what method should she employ? She decided to "sneak up" on her real concern. She began with two successful banquets. Her plan was working.

Personal Preparation

1. Read Esther 5:1-14. Recall how you have related to people in power. When you have been in authority, how have others related to you?
2. Consider what makes a good counselor or giver of advice. When have you benefited from excellent advice? When have you suffered through bad advice?
3. Take some time to contemplate the nature of grace. Have you ever tried to "engineer" a good outcome for yourself? Recall what happened, and then think about other times when the "good thing" came to you as a gift. Offer a prayer of thanks to God for those times.

Understanding

The school principal walked up to the soft-drink machine in the hallway and discovered that he did not have the proper change. Seeing a student walking his way, he called out: "Do you have change for a dollar, young man?"

The boy replied, "Yeah, I think so; just hold on an' I'll take a look-see."

The principal, annoyed at the student's disrespectful tone, said: "Son, that is no way to speak to your principal; so let's try it again. Now, do you have change for a dollar?"

The boy brought himself to attention and respectfully answered: "No, *Sir!*"

While this illustrates a situation mishandled by the principal, it points to the fragility of social interaction. We have daily opportunities to decide how we will approach others. Is diplomacy and tact always the best way? Are we required to be consistently candid and forthright, regardless of the potential consequences? Few of us face a situation as dangerous as Esther's. She approached the king, her husband, who held the power of life or death.

Cunning, Confrontational, or Careful?

In due course, as she had promised, Esther did make her approach to the king. She advanced very deliberately, keeping enough distance to allow the king to control the meeting. Esther had told Mordecai that her initial overture would be key to determining not only the success of her mission, but whether she would live or die (4:16). Most readers are not surprised when the king welcomes his queen. After all, this is a woman "admired by all who saw her" (2:15) and to whom the king was devoted (2:17), at least at one time.

Nevertheless, Esther could not presume upon the king's favor. She took every step with careful attention to protocol, waiting, responding, deferring. The king had always seemed willing to give to whatever was asked of him. He remained true to form on this occasion as well, offering Queen Esther half his empire before she even asked for anything (5:3). Next to the king's offer, Esther's request seems extraordinarily modest: a banquet for three, involving Esther, the king, and Haman, the chief royal advisor.

The king quickly agreed and the banquet took place immediately. Ahasuerus, apparently sensing that Esther had not yet made her real request, asked a second time. Again her husband offered half his kingdom. Surprisingly, Esther requested another banquet for the following night! However, she did agree to make her real request at the second dinner.

Some readers have praised Esther for her approach to the king, but others have chided her. Some have seen her plan as cunningly conceived; others have criticized her plan as deceptive, exploiting the king's weakness for food and drink and Haman's appetite for honor. Still others have warned against using Esther as a model because her approach appears passive and deferential rather than assertive and forthright.

Certainly Esther carried out a carefully considered plan, whether we choose to evaluate it positively or negatively. First and foremost, Esther followed protocol, working within the system. Some might call it "working the system," for Esther chose what we know to be the king's favorite environment, the banquet. On the other hand, apparently the king realized that Esther was working toward a goal that she had not yet revealed. Esther approached the king as a subject, but the king responded to her as the queen.

How should we approach one who has the power to decide, to grant a request? Children learn through trial and error how to approach their parents. Youthful approaches include tears, persistent pleading, bargaining, threat, and a myriad of strategies and plans. Children are generally far more inventive than adults in this endeavor. Young children generally adapt to what works, until they reach adolescence, when they usually adopt an adversarial approach to parental power.

We live in a time when the adversarial approach has gained popularity far beyond adolescence. Confronting power with power seems to have become the cultural—even global—norm. Out of this current belief that people should be confrontive and honest, some have criticized Esther as passive and weak.

I do not doubt that some benefits have resulted from aggressive confrontation, but there are costs as well. An adversarial clash does not always yield truth or lasting benefit. Such confrontations can create enmity that lasts far into the future. The Gospels show Jesus as one who approached power in a variety of ways, ranging from direct address to giving up his life. Perhaps Esther remains a woman worth watching, even if not emulating.

Happy and in Good Spirits

Haman left the banquet happy and in good spirits, celebrating his success with his family and friends. He had achieved all that this world can offer: wealth, children, power, honor, and influence. He possessed *almost* everything he wanted. Yet he was infuriated that Mordecai still would not bow down. Thus, Haman wanted the one thing that stood between him and complete happiness—to be rid of Mordecai.

Haman received his family's support in this. They advised him to prepare the instrument of Mordecai's destruction: "Let a gallows fifty cubits high be made, and in the morning tell the king to have Mordecai hanged on it" (5:14). This advice pleased Haman.

Once again in the narrative of Esther, advisors play a key role, though they seldom appear helpful in this story. The king's advisors were generally foolish or corrupt. They counseled him to get rid of Vashti and to destroy a "seditious" minority. Only in the process of selecting a new queen (2:2ff) can we say that the king received advice that produced a positive result. In this passage, Haman receives the counsel of those close to him. But his own friends and family served him no better than he had served the king.

Leadership cannot go it alone, of course. All leaders need people who can research, interpret, and counsel. Leaders need to see options and opportunities with more than their own eyes. But not all advice is helpful. This is the case in the New Testament when the ambivalent Pilate accepts the counsel of the chief priests to execute Jesus (Luke 23). Moreover, the advisors in the trial of Jesus are Jews like Jesus. Haman despised an alien, but the chief priests wanted to destroy one of their own. Kings, prelates, presidents, and all leaders are vulnerable. They may make poor decisions if they act alone, yet they may also make poor decisions if they accept the help and advice of others.

Just One Thing More
Haman had family, wealth, and power, but as he saw it, he lacked one thing, which proved to be his undoing. Wanting to "have it all" is familiar to us, but many of us have discovered that it is impossible to engineer our lives in ways that will assure everything will work out the way we want.

Jesus met a man who wanted it all, the one who asked: "What must I do to inherit eternal life?" (Mark 10:17). That man tried to achieve his goal through obedient piety. He, too, found out that he lacked still one thing. And he always would.

Both Haman and the man who met Jesus discovered that they could not grasp salvation. Neither good deeds nor evil plotting would make it happen. That may be the biggest shock of the Gospel, even to those of us trying to live out our faith. The narrative portrays Haman as greedy and evil, and it is apparent that he will lose everything, trying to get that one thing more. We consider that justice. For our part, we run into trouble at the same place as the good man in the Gospel. We can never do enough to gain eternal life: "When he heard this, he was shocked and went away grieving" (Mark 10:21).

There is more to the story, however: "For God so loved the world that he gave his only Son, so that everyone who believes in him may not perish but may have eternal life" (John 3:16). We cannot earn what we want. We will always lack that one thing. Yet we have been given it all through Jesus Christ. We need only to receive.

Discussion and Action

1. As a child, what special methods did you use to influence your parents or guardians? Can you remember a particular occasion when you succeeded or failed? If you have children, describe some forms of influence they have tried on you.

2. What methods have you used (or observed) to approach those who have the power to decide in your congregation? in your workplace? in the civic arena?

3. Diplomat Charles Colton once said: "Grant graciously what you cannot refuse safely, and conciliate those you cannot conquer." Do you agree, or disagree? In your opinion, to what extent is "working the system" faithful and necessary?

4. What faith values ought to inform the way we approach those who have the power to decide?

5. The desire to acquire more (power, money, influence, respect) fuels our economy, drives athletics, affects family dynamics, and impacts friendships. Yet the Christian faith affirms that in Christ, God has given us all we will ever want: abundant life. How does this truth relate to the positive dimension of ambition, of striving for excellence? How can we most faithfully live out our legitimate strivings?

6. What do you think the author means when he says: "Perhaps Esther remains a woman worth watching,

even if not emulating"? What aspects of Esther's character and actions would you like to emulate? What aspects would you prefer just to "watch"?

7. We need to test our perceptions of faith and life with the community. Yet the community can be wrong. How do you allow others to help you make decisions? Take some time in your group to discuss the role the community should play in testing (a) a call to a Christian vocation, (b) an interpretation of scripture, (c) our understanding of God, (d) God's will and purpose, (e) individual, prophetic voices that speak against the group.

8. Sometimes attempting to deal with systems and governments to effect change is an overwhelming task. Find out how your denomination witnesses to elected officials and government agencies on issues important to faith and civic life, such as crime, violence, war, and abortion.

7

Insomnia to Irony
Esther 6:1-13

Unable to fall asleep, Ahasuerus called for a reading of the official chronicles. Discovering that a good deed had gone unrewarded, he set in motion an ironic turn of events. None of us can be sure that things will always go as planned. Sometimes, in blessed irony, they work out better than we can imagine!

Personal Preparation

1. Reread Esther 5 before turning to Esther 6:1-13, where everything turns upside down for Haman. Recall a time when your own intentions went awry. How did you cope?
2. Looking back on the occasion, do you see God actively present, perhaps causing the reversal, maybe helping you adapt or enabling you to cope?
3. Most of us have had sleepless nights. What can such times teach about "controlling" and "letting go" in the context of one's spiritual life?

Understanding

A Troubled Night

Ahasuerus had one of those nights when sleep just would not come. Most of us have experienced his frustration, tossing and turning, unable to turn off the mind until the sheets become tangled and sweaty. Currently, conventional wisdom advises us to get up and do something to relax, such as read or watch television. The king may not have had the direct counsel of conventional wisdom, but he followed it nonetheless. He ordered his

servants to bring the royal chronicles for him to read. Quite likely the chronicles consisted of an extended list of national events
and royal actions. Such reading might well have induced sleep!

A Chance Discovery

As Ahasuerus read this chronicle of events, he came upon an
entry referring to a palace plot uncovered earlier in his reign.
Mordecai had announced a conspiracy by two royal officials to
assassinate the king. His report prevented the conspirators from
carrying out their scheme, presumably saving the king's life.

Ahasuerus asked his servants whether Mordecai had
received a reward for his loyalty. We might imagine irritation on
the part of the royal officials. Their sleep had been interrupted
to provide information to the king, information that surely
could have waited until the next morning. Thrilled or not, the
servants reported: "Nothing has been done for him" (6:3).

Interpreters over the centuries have suggested that the
king's troubled night did not happen merely by chance. God
must have disturbed his sleep on the night between Esther's
first and second banquet. A divine hand turned the page of the
royal chronicle to just the right place. (Actually, the Greek edition of Esther, which frequently includes explicit reference to
God's presence and action, reads: "God kept the king from
sleeping.") Perhaps God did lead the king to discover
Mordecai's long forgotten act of loyalty. The Hebrew text,
however, leaves that for us to decide.

The eyes of faith do give us a particular perspective on the
common events of everyday life, as well as on the major
events of human history. Faith enables us to suggest meaning
and purpose where others see only random events. And
where other perspectives might assume a closed system of
cause and effect, we see the universe as open to the active
presence of One unseen but not uninvolved. God makes the
universe less predictable from a human perspective, but more
trustworthy and forgiving. As a people who always fall short,
we can be thankful that we are not controlled by a world in
which every act brings an automatic consequence, every misstep a predictable judgment.

Identifying the presence of the divine touch is a matter of discernment and interpretation. Faithful Christians have and will
disagree about the discernible acts of God. We can mistakenly

declare, "Look! Here is the Messiah!" or "There he is!" (Matt. 24:23). Perhaps you have seen the cartoon by Rob Portlock. It shows a man sitting dejectedly in front of his loan officer at the bank. Behind a huge desk, the banker looks down with a smirk, saying: "Let me see if I have this right. You had a vision from on high that we should just forget about your $150,000 loan?"

Such presumptions not only hurt us, but they can bring pain to others as well. Most of us can recall times when a terminal disease or untimely death was attributed to "the will of God." However benign the intention, such an interpretation can confuse or anger people who have lost their health or their loved ones. It may create a picture of God as one who strikes down good people for unknowable reasons.

The history of the church is tarnished by the occasions when war has been interpreted as a divine call to arms, a crusade that carries the cross into battle. We look with horror as some in the Islamic tradition declare holy war in what appears to be a matter of personal or national interest. Yet we recognize the same stains on our clothing.

Nevertheless, we have been entrusted with eyes of faith. Perhaps God did indeed disturb the king's sleep, providing the opportunity for him to discover Mordecai's unrewarded act of loyalty. We can experience God's presence not only in our hearts, but also in the dramatic events of human history and in the routines of our daily lives. It remains for us to recognize the will of God—even in circumstances that are unclear or "shadowy"—and then live in relationship to it. Thus wrote seventeenth-century poet Henry Vaughn:

> There is in God (some say)
> A deep, but dazzling darkness; As men here
> Say it is late and dusky, because they
> See not all clear;
> O for that night! where I in him
> Might live invisible and dim.

An Ironic Twist

Whatever the reason for his sleeplessness, Ahasuerus did decide to rectify his oversight. Just then his chief of staff, Haman, entered the palace. Being one who always sought and took advice, the king asked Haman, "What shall be done for

the man whom the king wishes to honor?" (6:6). Assuming he
would be receiving the proposed honor, Haman sketched out
an elaborate ceremony, including a public parade. Predictably,
the king accepted the advice of his counselor and directed
Haman to carry out such a ceremony for Mordecai.

Mordecai, the Jew!

Haman carried out the king's command, but fell into deep
depression. The text says that Haman went home "mourning and
with his head covered" (6:12). His family and friends, previously
so supportive (5:14), turned on Haman. They announced that
Mordecai, apparently because he was Jewish, would prevail
against Haman. Haman would fall.

Haman's catastrophe portrays a classic case of irony in which
the consequences of an act are diametrically opposite to the orig-
inal intention. Haman intended his advice to provide a ceremony
of honor for himself. Instead, he was forced to lead the parade in
honor of his bitter enemy, Mordecai. Haman had been struck by
a painful reversal of fortune.

In biblical narrative, irony invites the reader to wonder about
the hidden presence of God. Certainly a situation of irony does
not require divine interpretation; it only provides the possibility for such. Yet irony often serves as a literary device of hope for
the oppressed. They can imagine their own situation and how
irony might play itself out for the good. Perhaps the evil plans
of the mighty will yet turn, bringing destruction to the oppressors instead of pain to the oppressed.

The Bible frequently identifies God as an actor in events
that could be termed ironic. Listen to the ironic reversals in
these passages, for instance:

> Why do the nations conspire,
>> and the people plot in vain? . . .
> He who sits in the heavens laughs;
>> the Lord has them in derision.
>> Psalm 2:1, 4

> He has brought down the powerful from their
>> thrones, and lifted up the lowly;
> he has filled the hungry with good things,
>> and sent the rich away empty.
>> Luke 1:52-53

We can see that Esther 6:1-13 serves as much more than the interlude between two banquets. At this point the fortunes of two main characters, Haman and Mordecai, begin to change. It happens through a series of "coincidences": a sleepless night, an inadvertent oversight, an early arrival at the palace, a serious misreading of a ruler's intention. The crisis has not been resolved, but according to Haman's wife, the direction is set (6:13).

Irony, prompted by the hand of God, encourages us to expect the new, no matter how dire the circumstances. Perhaps we can best live out of irony by learning to be expectant even amidst confusing, dazzling-dark situations, because we are assured of God's presence with us, even as we may wonder at the divine purpose. As writer John Fisher says, "Sometimes God answers us with questions—questions that leave us humbled, awed, speechless, weak and believing—believing not because we've found the answer, but because we've seen God. It doesn't matter that we have more questions now than when we started. It matters that we see God, for in the seeing, we discover that the truest answer to all our questions is to worship [our Lord.]"

Discussion and Action

1. From your personal preparation, share about a time when your intentions went awry (or when a plan unexpectedly came together). Looking back on the occasion, do you see God actively present, perhaps causing the reversal, maybe helping you adapt or enabling you to cope?

2. What things tend to give you a bad night? How do you handle sleeplessness? What remedies have worked for you that you could suggest for others?

3. In *Now and Then,* Frederick Buechner writes: "The word that God speaks to us is always an incarnate word—a word spelled out to us not alphabetically, in syllables, but enigmatically, in events." What is your response to this statement? Can you name happenings that you now perceive as God working in history? Some have suggested that events such as the end of the Vietnam War or the fall of the Berlin Wall should be interpreted as divine irony.

4. Many of us have heard others suggest that God's will or action was connected with an event. Identify a time

when you questioned (at least silently) this interpretation of divine intervention. What generated your
doubts? Begin to identify some *criteria* by which your
group would consider the hand of God as a likely factor in the course of events.

5. Many people living in circumstances of political, religious, or social oppression yearn for irony. They hope
for the plans of the oppressors to twist and catch themselves in the net of their own schemes. Can you recall a
situation in which events took just such an ironic twist?
Do you see the hand of God involved in such reversals
of fortune in world events?

6. How do you respond to the closing quotation by
John Fisher? What is your own experience with
"believing without answers"?

7. The author refers to the presumptuous interpretations
sometimes given when people get sick or die. What
"pious nothings" have you heard? Brainstorm
together for a few minutes about more meaningful
and helpful things that can be done or said at such
times. Determine to use your ideas in the future.

8

The Dangerous Banquet
Esther 6:14—7:10

Esther, Haman, and the king gather for the second banquet requested by Esther. This banquet is fraught with danger for all the participants. What will Esther reveal? How will the king and Haman respond?

Personal Preparation

1. Esther 6:14—7:10 narrates the events of the second banquet requested by the queen. How does this banquet stand in relationship to the first dinner (5:1-8) and the king's sleepless night (6:1-9)? Notice, for example, the king repeats his offer to Esther to give her half his kingdom (5:3,6; 7:2).

2. Here we will look at leadership and risk. Dramatic moments can challenge leaders with the risk of life or death. Recall some of those great moments of leadership in history. Also notice some of the risks that test you and those leaders close to you. They may not make headlines, but they require courage.

Understanding

Esther's Petition
The narrative cuts short Haman's discussion with his family and friends: "While they were still talking with him, the king's eunuchs arrived and hurried Haman off to the banquet that Esther had prepared" (6:14). This very first verse introduces an element of urgency. The story has featured many types of banquets, official banquets, national banquets, women's banquets,

private banquets. Now Haman is summoned to a dangerous banquet, the banquet that may appear benign but turns out deadly.

The narrative continues at a quick pace. Ahasuerus immediately renews his inquiry: "What is your petition, Queen Esther?" At the first banquet Esther promised that she would fully answer the king's question at this meal, and so she will. Now, however, the narrative slows down. As in 5:1-4, we find Esther very carefully deferential in her approach to the king. She states her request: "Let my life be given me, that is my petition—and the lives of my people, that is my request" (7:3).

Esther went on to explain to the king that she and her people had been "sold" to be killed. She expressed her anguish, giving no hint as to the person who betrayed them. Esther added that had the betrayal involved anything less than death, she would have kept her mouth shut.

Not unexpectedly, the king did not know what the queen was talking about: "Who is he, and where is he?" (7:5). Esther's uncharacteristically abrupt response betrayed her true emotion: "This wicked Haman!"

Leadership

The story of Esther gives the reader the opportunity to explore several dimensions of leadership. The royal advisors alone represent leadership that is at times appropriate, incompetent, and evil. The king's leadership ranges from uncommonly inept to fairly benign. He regularly consulted others before acting, but he uncritically accepted their recommendation. In so doing, he foolishly deposed Queen Vashti in order to protect family values in the Persian empire. Even more tragically the king accepted Haman's disguised counsel concerning a treasonous minority in the kingdom. In so doing the king permitted the decree of death against the Jews.

Not all the king's passive leadership produced tragic results. Following the recommended selection process, the king appointed Esther as queen. And, accepting the advice of Haman, the king ordered a ceremony of honor for Mordecai, which began the downfall of his chief of staff.

The two royal courtiers, Mordecai and Haman, exercised their leadership in the interest of themselves or their people. Mordecai used his political smarts for his people when he instructed Esther to hide her religious identity in order to become queen. Then he persuaded her to intercede with the king in the face of the death decree to Jews. Haman, on the other hand, worked hard to manipulate the royal power so as to enhance his own position and to destroy his enemies. Eventually he was caught in his own trap.

Most importantly, the narrative recognizes the remarkable leadership of Esther. Her leadership exhibits a mature mix of prudence and risk. Esther did not exactly begin that way. She simply followed the counsel of her guardian, Mordecai, and her patron, Hegai. But once Esther seized the initiative herself (4:16), she did not give it up. The narrative provides us little direct access to Esther's thoughts and emotions, only her words and actions. What we see is her careful work within the palace milieu on behalf of her people threatened with annihilation. We know Esther realized the risk. Apparently she gave herself the best possibility of success. Then she acted.

History provides numerous examples of those who have led in the tradition of Esther. Sometimes such leadership happens in the public eye, such as Nelson Mandela in South Africa and Mohandas Gandhi in India. More often, careful, but risk-filled leadership has been exercised by history's unnamed saints. Such leadership can be dramatic, such as leadership in America's "underground railroad" and European leaders that hid Jews from the Nazis. We must not forget the stories in our own communities and congregations, however, where leaders have protected women and children from abuse, kept congregations from polarizing, and prevented urban gangs from going to war.

Haman's Demise
The king erupted in anger when the queen identified Haman as the betrayer. He left the room perhaps to cool off (7:7), though we can't tell from the story with whom the king is most angry; it might have been Esther, or it could have been Haman. Haman assumed that he was the one. He threw himself at the queen, pleading for mercy. At that opportune, or inopportune, moment the king returned to the room. He found Haman in what the king considered a "compromising" position on Esther's couch. The king accused Haman of sexual assault and ordered him executed (7:9). In a final twist

of irony, Haman was executed for sexual assault, a crime he did not commit, on the gallows Haman himself had prepared for Mordecai.

The issue of justice draws this narrative toward its conclusion, beginning with the execution of Haman. Haman's guilt was not in doubt, if not for sexual assault then for plotting the annihilation of the Jews in Persia. Though capital punishment is not a serious issue in this narrative, it remains on the contemporary agenda. The end of the twentieth century in the United States has witnessed the return of execution as the punishment for a number of crimes, usually involving murder. Proponents of capital punishment no longer agree on execution as a deterrent to crime. Execution has regained popularity as retribution, "an eye for an eye." Surveys show that about the same percentage of Christians support capital punishment as we find in the general population.

Some people are born leaders. They take leadership by their own initiative. But many more people become leaders by necessity, when a situation arises that calls upon all their resources. Which of us, like Esther, can take leadership, not to elevate ourselves, but to make justice? We may never know. The moment may not come for us personally. But we can look around our congregations and communities and quickly see the Esthers among us and pray for the willingness and courage to be a leader when the time arises.

Discussion and Action

1. The theme of leadership continues throughout this narrative. At this point we want to look particularly at the risks inherent in leadership. Who are some heroes from the past who have risked their lives in leadership? Think of national and international political leadership. Remember also some of the heroes of faith from the broad stream of Christian history and from your denominational branch of that history. What was the particular goal for which they were willing to "lay down their lives" for their brothers and sisters?
2. Elements of risk also exist in leadership in everyday life. The risk may not involve a matter of life and death, but leaders in the family, congregation, workplace, and civic affairs face decisions that risk reputa-

tion, friendship, even employment; anger, criticism, even attack. Recount some of those stories, perhaps your own.

3. Some feel that we have developed an unfair and unwarranted antagonism and distrust of leadership, that we are quick to criticize and basically unforgiving. Do you agree? If so, why has that attitude emerged?

4. This narrative assumes the existence and use of the death penalty. Voices and traditions in the Christian community continue to raise objections. Capital punishment can be discussed as a secular matter of deterrence or retribution, but our faith commitment calls on us to consider the matter in the light of Jesus and the New Testament. What New Testament texts inform your perspective on the death penalty? Review your denomination's position if there is one. Discuss it.

5. Identify different styles of leadership. Which of these styles require risk? Which kind of leadership do you prefer in a president of the country, in a business person, in a teacher, in a pastor, in a parent? How are these styles of leadership the same or different?

6. Name the leadership qualities you see in people in your covenant group or in the congregation.

9

A Second Decree
Esther 8:1—9:17

Haman is dead, but the decree of destruction still stands. Esther obtained from the king the right to draft a new decree to counter the decree of annihilation of the Jews; consequently, she writes a decree authorizing violent self-defense for any Jew who is attacked.

Personal Preparation

1. Read Esther 8:1—9:17. What feelings do you have, seeing Haman and his sons finally getting their "comeuppance"?
2. Virtually every week brings news stories of the violence epidemic. Clip some of them from the newspaper and be ready to share them with your group.
3. In connection with this text, we will look not only at exploitative and criminal violence, but violence on behalf of a just cause. Think about for what or for whom you could kill.

Understanding

Ancient Chinese proverb: "If thine enemy wrong thee, buy each of his children a drum." At first glance, this may seem a rather mild form of retaliation—until we let it sink in for a moment.

That focuses the issue. Human beings immediately think of ways to get back at the ones who hurt them. Thus, in this story, Mordecai obtained the right of self-defense, but the violence escalated far beyond that.

Mordecai's Appointment

Note that Esther 8:1—9:17 functions as the counterpart to chapter 3. In the third chapter, Ahasuerus promotes Haman to the position of prime minister, in spite of Mordecai's work to thwart an assassination plot. Following his promotion Haman persuaded the king to approve a death decree against a subversive group, which turned out to be the Jews. Each step in that chapter has its parallel in this selection.

Chapter 3 reports Haman's promotion to "prime minister," the most powerful position among the royal advisors. But his abuse of that power brought his downfall and death. With Haman gone, Mordecai re-entered the story. Based on information supplied by Esther (8:1), King Ahasuerus appointed him to Haman's government office. With that appointment, the balance of power shifted from one minority in the empire to another.

Power in the political realm can shift and move quickly, as happens in this narrative. Such sudden shifts may occur whether the officials have obtained their position by election, inheritance, appointment, or violence. The tenuous character of political power prompts officials to engage in a variety of efforts to consolidate their control. Quite often the endeavor to "stay in office" turns the attention of officials away from their responsibilities and misdirects their energy toward the elimination of anyone who might pose a threat.

Ironically, such political self-protection frequently results in the loss of power, as it did with Haman. Even though it is popular (and sometimes accurate) to blame the officeholder for a distorted self- interest, in North America the electorate too often participates in such perversion of the political process. We desire those who will put principle over politics. Yet we voters often make our individual self-interest a higher priority than the integrity of the candidate. Then we wonder where all the "Hamans" come from, those who conspire to insure their own re-election at the expense of governing for the common good.

A Second Decree

One important thread in the story remained unresolved. While Haman no longer posed a threat, the death decree against the Jews remained law. With that concern the queen again approached the king with a request. Esther's approach this time was more servile and intense than it had been earlier: She fell at the king's feet, weeping and pleading (8:3). Once again Ahasuerus invited Esther to speak. Earlier Esther requested a banquet. Not so this time. This time she directly told the king she wanted the death decree revoked.

That could not happen. In this story, a decree, once stamped with the king's seal, could not be revoked, could not be declared "unconstitutional" or in some other way overturned. If the Jews were to be saved, another way had to be found to neutralize the decree. At this point in the narrative, the king addresses not just Esther, but Queen Esther and Mordecai (8:7). Ahasuerus gave them the same privilege that he extended to Haman (see 3:10-11). They could formulate any decree they chose and stamp it irrevocably with the royal seal.

Mordecai took charge. He wrote a decree allowing the Jews to defend themselves against anyone who attacked them and/or their family (8:11). Some translations read as if Mordecai's decree permitted the Jews to kill the women and children of their enemies. Most current interpreters insist that is a mistranslation. Mordecai formulated a self-defense decree against those who sought to destroy all the Jews—men and women, elderly and young (see 3:13).

Violence remains one of our most difficult issues, especially when we consider our desire to defend ourselves and our families from unjust or senseless attack. For the most part, the legal tradition in North America allows for the use of violence in self-defense, extending that to the protection of family and even neighbor. Many Christians, however, question any use of violence by the disciples of Jesus. They understand following the Way to include a commitment to giving up one's own life rather than taking the life of another, even an enemy: "No one has greater love than this, to lay down one's life for one's friends" (John 15:13).

Even Christians who cannot completely renounce violence recognize that the claim of self-defense can be employed to justify almost any action. Friedrich Nietzsche, Hitler's philosopher-hero who glorified violence, said: "How good bad music and bad reasons sound when we march against an enemy." We know that virtually all wars have been started under the banner of self-defense or some other "good-sounding" cause.

The problem of justifying violence extends far beyond war. Claims of physical threat accompany situations ranging from domestic violence to gang violence. The inability to sort out aggressive violence from self-defense constitutes another reason why many Christian groups insist that we must find alternatives to violence in all situations. Many hope we will direct more of our energies toward understanding others rather than preparing to fight them. "If we could read the secret history of our enemies," said Henry Wadsworth Longfellow, "we should find in each [person's] life sorrow and suffering enough to disarm all hostility."

In this narrative the decree authorizing self-defense results in universal rejoicing within the anxious Jewish community (8:15). Mordecai, wearing the royal robes of prime minister, appeared in the midst of his happy people. The text says that the self-defense decree created an incredible reversal. Whereas many, like Esther, had previously hidden their Jewish identity, now many were claiming to be Jews out of fear for their lives.

Destroying the Enemies
In chapter nine the Jews seem to take the initiative in exacting revenge, not at all the intention of the self-defense decree. Even if the surrealistic quality of the scene reduces the horror, it reminds us of what can happen when violence is unleashed even in self-defense. The oppressed can very quickly become the oppressor. The rage of the victims can be translated into uncontrolled vengeance. Years of domestic abuse can generate violence that turns not only on the abuser, but on other family members as well. Likewise, generations of political oppression can erupt in a revolution that will not stop short of annihilation.

The threat of nuclear annihilation has diminished enough that the words of President Kennedy sound like a bygone era:

> Today, every inhabitant of this planet must contemplate the day when it may no longer be habitable. Every man, woman, and child lives under a nuclear sword of Damocles, hanging by the slenderest of threads, capable of being cut at any moment by accident, miscalculation, or madness. The weapons of war must be abolished before they abolish us.

Nevertheless, nuclear weapons remain the ultimate weapon of retaliation sought by terrorist groups as well as governments of countries large and small. One would wish for simple solutions to stop all violence—individual, social, and international. Though easy solutions do not exist, the search for alternatives to violence and efforts to intervene prior to violence do continue. Even if we feel powerless to influence world events, we can confront violence at the most personal levels in our lives, day by day. We can identify safe shelters for those victimized by domestic abuse. We can work to end easy access to the weapons of violence. We can support international efforts for economic and political intervention in circumstances of oppression. Although these and other efforts remain controversial, no one can deny that violence continues to infect the home, spreading a horrible decay across the land. It is the number one preventable cause of death in North America.

Discussion and Action

1. Look at the second item in personal preparation. Share any newspaper clippings you have brought with you, and discuss some of the causal factors in each case. Then consider what kinds of alternative actions could have been taken to avoid the violent "solution." Also, pray for the specific acts of violence you found. Pray for both victims of violence and those who are violent toward others.

2. Focus on Personal Preparation, number 3, and respond to this quotation by William James: "We are all ready to be savage in some cause. The difference between a good [person] and a bad one is the choice of the cause." Do you agree? What is your own experience with choosing and "fighting" for a cause?

3. We usually find it easier to talk about violence in general than in particular cases. When, if ever, is violence justified? Consider inviting a person who deals with domestic or gang violence into the discussion. Follow up by naming ways to participate in alternatives to violence.

4. We frequently focus our discussions about violence on the extreme "what if" situations, such as, What if an

assailant attacked my child and I could only prevent my child's murder by shooting the assailant? Lay the extremes aside, knowing you will do the best you can in such a situation. Instead, lay out your affirmations of faith in relationship to violence. How can you be proactive in living out these affirmations in your home, your church, the community, the world?

5. The author states: "We know that virtually all wars have been started under the banner of self-defense or some other 'good-sounding' cause." What good-sounding causes can you recall in the history of our nation?

6. Look at your denominational statements on violence, nonviolence, and war. What parts of these statements do you find helpful? Are you dissatisfied with any aspects of your denomination's official position? Are there issues of violence that ought to receive additional and wider discussion?

7. Make a list of groups of people who scare you. What is it about these groups that generates fear in you? Seek out information about the groups. If the groups are in your community, find out who could be a resource in learning about these groups. For instance, if gangs make you fearful, call and find out about gang recovery programs.

8. What organizations and programs in your community are trying to find alternatives to violence or ways to intervene and break the circle of violence? Does your school system have a program that teaches the children conflict management and mediation? Could one be started through the schools, a community organization, or even a park district? What is the community relations department of the police doing to help?

Decide on one way your group or some members of the group can work constructively toward violence prevention.

The Festival
Esther 9:18—10:3

Mourning turns to feasting, grief becomes gladness. Because Esther and Mordecai had managed to save their people, a festival was proclaimed for the benefit of all future generations.

Personal Preparation

1. Read the final chapters of Esther and look up additional material on the festival of Purim. What festivals and feasts are important in your church?
2. What traditions and celebrations do you happily recall from your childhood—in your family or church community? Which of these involved eating?
3. Christmas and Easter are the most celebrative Christian festivals. Families celebrate birthdays and anniversaries. Who in your church, family, or neighborhood has special reason to celebrate as you study this chapter? Remembering them in prayer and person, think about ways you might be able to add to their enjoyment on their special day.
4. Make a list of new learnings you have gleaned from this study of Esther. Be prepared to share them with the group.

Understanding

The Book of Banquets

We have seen that Esther is a book of banquets. The narrative began with a series of feasts thrown by the king and queen. In the middle of the story, two banquets requested by Esther exposed the plot of Haman to destroy the Jews, thus averting the crisis (Esther 5—7). Prior to those two banquets, fast replaced feast as Esther decided what she would do about the developing disaster (4:16). Not surprisingly the story concludes with a feast, Purim, a Jewish holiday in which the people eat together and send gifts of food to one another.

At the beginning of our study, we looked at the role eating, in general, plays in our life together. The story of Esther ends, however, with a festival in celebration of a *particular* event, the deliverance of the Jews from a decree of death. This calls to mind a different aspect of eating together, one in which the focus is not only on the gathering but also on remembering a common story.

Such festivals of food and remembrance are crucial in forming and maintaining the life of the faith community. The meal central to the Christian tradition is the Lord's Supper, or Eucharist, in which the family of faith eats and remembers the death and resurrection of Jesus Christ. Some participate in this feast as a regular part of Sunday morning worship. Others celebrate the Lord's Supper on certain special occasions, often in connection with Holy Week and Easter. Some communities share the bread and cup only, while others expand this to include a full fellowship meal.

The Lord's Supper is the feast that forms our community and unites all Christians, but it can become an occasion for division, as well. Some Christians feel so strongly about their understanding of the "correct" way to celebrate the Lord's Supper that they refuse to share it with those who follow different ways. Then the Lord's meal is hardly an occasion in which people "send gifts of food to one another" (9:19).

Purim

In this concluding portion of Esther, we discover that the festival of Purim gets its name from "pur." This casting of lots decided the day on which to carry out the death decree against the Jews (3:7). The account further explains why Purim became a two-day festival: the Jews in the villages throughout the provinces of Persia rested for the holiday of Purim on the fourteenth day of Adar, whereas the residents of the city of Susa made the fifteenth the feast day (9:17-19). Therefore, Mordecai declared that Purim would be celebrated on both

days. Adar is the twelfth month of the Jewish calendar, rough-
ly concurrent with our month of March.

The Jewish community still gathers for Purim today, usually in mid-March, depending on the lunar calendar. In many
synagogues the festival takes on the atmosphere of a party.
Participants dress up in costumes representing the different
characters in the story of Esther. Using noisemakers, those
gathered try to drown out the name of evil Haman every time
it is spoken in the oral reading of the story.

Although a reading of the book of Esther is the central fea-
ture of the festival, the story is more than just a biblical narrative. The characters have become symbols of all evil oppo-
nents and delivering heroes throughout Jewish history.
Unfortunately, "Haman" has reappeared far too often in that
history. *Pogrom* is the word for the periodic efforts to destroy
or displace the Jewish population in a local or regional area.
Ethnic cleansing has entered the vocabulary more recently to
describe the same activity, a victimizing of minority popula-
tions. In light of this constant threat, we can understand the
joy of remembering those times when the enemy was
destroyed and the oppressed delivered. The narrative twice
urges subsequent generations not to forget the festival of
Purim (9:28, 31).

Concluding Scene

The story ends applauding the accomplishments of Ahasuerus
and Mordecai. Mordecai had become next in rank to the king
himself, and the acts of Mordecai were so renowned that they
apparently were recorded in the royal chronicles of Persia. He
became a powerful and popular Jewish leader. (Esther, hero of
the deliverance, has disappeared from the conclusion of the
story).

The Jewish community has often sought to achieve some
measure of political stature as a minority in various lands, in
order to lessen the chance of victimization by prejudice. That
hope has occasionally been realized. Nehemiah 11:24 records
the name of a Jew, Pethahiah, who may have served as advisor in the Persian court. And one of the greatest leaders in
Jewish history, Maimonides (A.D. 1135—2104), may have risen
to high political office in the Moslem empire of the Orient.
Jews have a long history of cooperative participation in the

lands where they live, contributing not only political and business acumen, but producing brilliant physicians, scholars, writers, and musicians.

A Hostile Reception

In spite of the blessings many receive from reading and studying Esther, the story has always had its detractors. Perhaps you have heard Luther's well-known comment about the book: "I am so hostile to it that I wish it did not exist." His attitude echoes throughout the history of biblical interpretation. The book's inclusion in the canon (the accepted, authoritative books of the Bible) was in dispute well into the fourth century. Church councils at Hippo (A.D. 393) and Carthage (A.D. 397) clearly accepted its canonicity but, as Luther's comment illustrates, that did not settle the dispute.

The absence of an explicit mention of God is a frequently voiced objection to the story of Esther. As noted earlier, the Greek edition of the story, used in the official translations of the Roman Catholic Church, does refer to God. The divine name does not appear in the Hebrew text, though, which is the basis for Protestant and Jewish translations. That absence ultimately can provide readers an opportunity to become participants in the story, discerning the presence of God as they can. Such practice at discernment can help us identify God's presence in the national and personal events of our own day.

Other Christians have objected to the violence portrayed in the narrative, a concern frequently raised along with other parts of the Old Testament and in parts of the New Testament, especially those picturing the "last days." In Esther, the problem lies not in violence alone, but in the attitude about revenge against enemies (Esther 8—9).

The problem of Christianity and violence is one that continues to require discussion as we seek to live as disciples of the One who gave up his life rather than take the life of the enemy. The story of Esther will serve the church well if it prompts the community to discuss the issue of violence.

Discussion and Action

1. From Personal Preparation, number one, tell about additional material you've gathered on the festival of

Purim. How does the idea of celebrating an enemy's downfall strike you?

2. Referring to the second item in Personal Preparation, spend some time telling about traditions in your home or at church that you recall from your childhood. Then identify present-day festivals in your family and congregation that are designed to excite the memory.

3. The author points out that the absence in Esther of a direct reference to God may provide readers an opportunity to discern the *presence* of God as they can. Did you experience the presence of God in the story? Where? What prompted your experience?

4. Luther's hostility? What reservations do you have about including Esther in the biblical canon? What can Christians learn from careful study of this story? What new things have you learned from your study of Esther?

5. It may not be enough to celebrate the beginning of a congregation every fifty or hundred years. Some congregations have begun a tradition of an annual "founders day," so they can retell the story of the congregation every year. Could your congregation or family do more to ensure that the next generation learns your story? Brainstorm for practical action ideas.

6. Talk about your experiences of celebrating the Lord's Supper. What role does remembrance play in this event? When have you known division, and when unity, around observance of the Lord's Supper?

7. Minorities that seek to live easily as a part of the community often almost become invisible groups. You may be working with or living near a Jewish family without knowing it. Make an attempt to become acquainted with the Jewish community in your area. For example, you might invite a rabbi or a lay member of the synagogue to talk with your group about the festival of Purim (and also about the presence of the Jewish community in your area and local issues that concern Jews). Or attend a service at the synagogue—if not Purim, then one of the weekly sabbath services. Also invite Jewish friends to join you for worship.

Suggestions for Sharing and Prayer

This material is designed for covenant groups that spend one hour sharing and praying together, followed by one hour of Bible study. The following suggestions will help relate the group's sharing and praying time to their study of *Esther*. You'll find session-by-session ideas, as well as ideas that relate to all ten meetings. General resources for sharing and prayer then follow. Rev. Cathy Myers Wirt has developed these creative ideas. Use those you find most helpful, and bring your own ideas for sharing and worshiping together in your covenant group.

1. Every Day a Banquet

❏ Begin by forming or renewing your covenant together as a group. Use the Covenant Expectations given under General Sharing and Prayer Resources, or develop your own covenant.

❏ Take some time to talk together about how you will conduct your meetings during this study. Also decide on the "rituals" (see General Sharing and Prayer Resources) you will observe as a group during the ten weeks. Who will be responsible for the various parts of this process, week by week?

❏ If you are going to learn a prayer song together, begin teaching it. You might also take some time to sing hymns together (from your church hymnal) that give you courage. Or simply read the words aloud. See the end of this section for selected hymns. When in your life did you need the most courage? How did you experience the help of God and/or friends during this time?

❑ This might be a good meeting time to make sandwiches for a shelter. You have so much text to discuss that you could use the activity as a break time. Or you could talk about the text while making sandwiches.

❑ Name scriptures that give you courage and read them to each other. Here's a way to do it: have one person at a time sit in the middle of your group circle. Then read each person's favorite scripture to him or her in unison.

2. Incompetent Leadership

❑ When have you been in the uncomfortable position of having to take a stand and risk appearing foolish? To facilitate candid sharing about this, have volunteers do pudding paintings. Take instant pudding mixed with milk and put a few tablespoons on a sheet of freezer paper in front of volunteers. (Waxed butcher paper is available in the meat department or in the paper products area of your grocery store.)

Participants can use this mixture to finger-paint a scene of a time when they felt at risk, perhaps in a leadership position. (Or really take a risk and do a tongue painting of that scene!) No one is good at this task, and it makes us laugh with each other, thereby taking some of the fear out of the stories we are portraying. It can be fun to watch, too. But, of course, don't try to force anyone to take part.

❑ Draw your family tree and make special note of the "women of high courage" in your family. Share with one another the stories of these women. Which of their personal qualities do you most admire?

❑ On construction paper, draw two tables—one for the family in which you currently live and one for the family in which you grew up. Using these pictures, describe how decisions were/are made around these tables. Who speaks first and/or most? Who usually doesn't have a voice? What patterns can you discern and talk about?

❑ If you had to make a tough decision next week, name the three people whose advice you would seek out. Explain your choices.

❑ Obedience is a factor in this text. Draw an imaginary line running the length of the room. Label one end of the room absolutely perfect and the other end of the room absolutely at odds.

In how I spend my time, I am in obedience to God.
In how I spend my resources, I am in obedience to God.
In how I listen to others, I am in obedience to God.
In how I choose my words, I am in obedience to God.
In how I express my sexuality, I am in obedience to God.
In how I care for myself, I am in obedience to God.

As the six statements above are read aloud, move to a place on the line that indicates your response. Then re-gather in a circle, and talk about why you chose your particular places on the "obedience line." Share about areas in your life where you feel a need to increase your obedience to God. Pray for one another in these areas.

3. A Queen with Charisma

❑ Visualize a time when you have been in the minority, and take a few moments to feel the emotions this brings up. Either lead group members in a guided meditation about a particular minority situation. Or simply share together about memories of being in a minority, either by virtue of who you are (race, gender, class, etc.) or because you held beliefs that differed from the group.

❑ Using clay, make two shapes that express (1) how it feels to be in the minority in a group and (2) how it feels to be in the majority. Tell about your sculptures.

❑ Do you have a leader in race relations in your community? What special leadership qualities and charisma do you see in this person? Work together on writing him or her a letter of appreciation.

❑ Offer prayers for each other, naming situations in which each person needs extra courage for the week ahead. Consider using the ancient custom of "laying on of hands" while praying for each group member in turn.

4. Injustice Intended

❑ Reflect on a long- running feud or fight that has plagued your family and/or church. Share these conflicts by writing a phrase or drawing a symbol of the conflict and placing these items in a basket at the center of the circle. Then lift them up—literally—in prayer. One person could pray for the concerns as he or she holds the basket, or pass the basket around and take turns praying.

❑ Create body sculptures to display what conflict looks like. Designate one person at a time as the artist and allow him or her to use the group as their medium of creation. The artist tells the group members how to stand together and what to do in order to become the conflict-sculpture. Then the artist explains the body sculpture to the group members while they stand/sit/lie in their sculpted positions.

❑ Mary Ann Evans, a nineteenth-century English novelist, wrote: "Who shall put his finger on the work of justice, and say, 'It is there'? Justice is like the kingdom of God: it is not outside of us as a fact; it is within us as a great yearning." When have you felt the yearning Evans speaks of? What were the circumstances at the time?

❑ Sing hymns to each other and read scriptures to one another. Choose hymns and readings that give you courage in the face of evil.

5. A Defining Moment

❑ Describe to each other times when you have been in the right place at the right time to make a difference to someone. Also tell stories of times when someone else was in the right place at the right time to help you. How would you describe God's presence at such "critical moments"?

❑ We often find it easier to talk about God's presence in the hearts of individuals than to talk about the acts of God in public history. The Bible encourages us to do the latter as well as the former. Where do you see God's presence in current international events? What "grist" for prayer do you find here?

❑ List all the resources you have at your disposal—material and spiritual. Who might need those gifts? How is God calling you to use what you have power over in your life?

❑ On a sheet of paper (one for each group member), write the phrase "I saw your faith in action when you . . . ." Put the name of a group member on each of the sheets and pass these sheets around the room, giving each participant a chance to write on each one. You may choose to read the responses aloud, either having people read their own or having people read them to each other.

❑ Cut out heart-shaped pieces of paper and write a phrase such as "Take Heart" on them. Then write a scripture of encouragement on each one. You may give these to members of your congregation or give them to your elders or pastor to take to hospital or nursing home patients.

6. Approaching Authority

❑ What would you name as the best advice you've ever received? What was so special about this wise counsel? What was the *worst* advice you've ever been given?

❑ Write a letter to the President or send him e-mail about a concern your group has. Or offer a note of appreciation for something he has done.

❑ Take eight strips of paper, each measuring 1" x 8", and divide the slips into two groups of four. On four of the slips, write an issue or a place that causes you deep despair. On the other four, write places or ways that you know deep and abiding hope. Weave these strips into the covenant cross symbol representing this covenant program. (You can secure the slips with an X of tape on the back of the woven area.) Share about your crosses with each other, telling how despair and hope commingle in your lives.

❑ Lift up silent prayers for situations in the world that you see as having no solution. Envision Christ standing in that place. Look into his face. What do you see in his eyes? Lift up prayers of gratitude for places or situations where you have seen reconciliation and healing. Envision Christ standing in that place. Look into his face. What do you see in his eyes?

❑ Create a litany with the repeated phrase "I see pain . . . [fill in the blank]. I see hope . . . [fill in the blank]." Ask people to say both to remember that pain and hope co-exist in faithful living.

7. Insomnia to Irony

❑ Share about your sleep patterns. Are you a light sleeper or a heavy sleeper? What keeps you awake? What helps you fall asleep? When has sleep been a great blessing to you?

❑ Using a small paper bag and pictures cut from magazines, glue the pictures on the inside and outside of the bag to depict a time when what you may have looked like on the outside was quite different from how you felt on the inside. On the inside of the bag, glue the pictures or words that show how you felt. On the outside of the bag, glue the items that symbolize your outward appearance at the time. Interpret your bags for each other.

❑ What ironic moments do you recall in your life experience or in your observations? What makes an event or statement ironic?

❑ When we become frightened in confusing situations, it is easy to stop breathing or breathe in a shallow manner. Introduce the concept of breath prayers. Choose a scripture or phrase of hope and divide it in half. While breathing in deeply, say one half of the phrase. And while breathing out completely, say the last half of the phrase. Do this slowly and for at least twenty repetitions. Use breath prayers daily this week and report to the group about your experience at your next meeting.

❑ As a group, have a prayer vigil. This might last for a five-to ten-hour period during the week. One person could take a half-hour shift and then call the next person on the list. Or you might meet as a group for an hour or two of silence, praying for a special need in your congregation.

❑ Purchase some inexpensive "poppers" from a party store (they make a loud pop and shoot confetti out the end). Standing in a line or circle, name people of courage you have known, and then pull the string on your popper (point the poppers upward!) as you celebrate their witness.

8. The Dangerous Banquet

❑ Who would you name as your hero(es)? Refer to both contemporary and historic figures. What gives these people heroic qualities for you?

❑ Tell about a time when you were able to be a hero to a younger person. What role did your faith play in this mentoring situation? In what ways would you like to improve in your ability to model a risky faith commitment?

❑ Share the story of an unjust death within your circle of friends and family. How did you grieve this loss differently from other deaths/losses? If you could ask God one question about this death, what would that question be?

❑ Using pen and paper, draw pictures that portray your feelings and thoughts about the death penalty. Share these, remembering that people of faith stand on both sides of the death penalty debate. Why do we feel the way we do? Explore where some of your feelings may have come from on this issue.

9. A Second Decree

❑ Share a story of the most violent act you have ever seen in person. How did this affect your sense of safety in the world? Did it change your behavior in any way?

❑ Collect grooming items for a local shelter for battered people. Pray over the items by touching them and passing them around the circle, and pray for the people who will receive them.

❑ As members of the human family, all of us participate in violence of one kind or another. Write confessional prayers about where you are or have been involved in violence.

10. The Festival

❑ Read the story of Esther, or large portions of it, as Jews do on Purim. "Boo" the villains and cheer the heroes with noisemakers.

❑ If it is your tradition, and you can do so without priest or pastor, celebrate Communion together.

❑ Create a litany using the phrase, "I am changed because of covenant group . . ." (fill in the blank). Then spend time sharing which part of the Esther story had the most impact on you and your life of faith.

❑ Give each other a gift of scripture chosen specifically for each member. For example, I might choose to give a special Psalm to one member of the group, a passage from one of the Epistles to another. Ask each person to come prepared to give a scripture to another group member. Or you might draw names, with each person offering a scripture gift for one other person.

❑ Sing together the hymns you have identified as courage-giving. Then gather in a circle and lay hands on one another, offering prayers of courage and dedication.

General Sharing and Prayer Resources

Forming a Covenant Group

Covenant Expectations

Covenant-making is significant throughout the biblical story. God made covenants with Noah, Abraham, and Moses. Jeremiah spoke about God making a covenant with the people, "written on the heart." In the New Testament, Jesus was identified as the mediator of the New Covenant, and the early believers lived out of covenant relationships. Throughout history people have lived in covenant relationship with God and within community.

Christians today also covenant with God and make commitments to each other. Such covenants help believers live out their faith. God's empowerment comes to them as they gather in covenant communities to pray and study, share and receive, reflect and act.

People of the Covenant is a program that is anchored in this covenantal history of God's people. It is a network of covenantal relationships. Denominations, districts or regions, congregations, small groups, and individuals all make covenants. Covenant group members commit themselves to the mission statement, seeking to become more:

—biblically informed so they better understand the revelation of God;

—globally aware so they know themselves to be better connected with all of God's world;

—relationally sensitive to God, self, and others.

The Burlap Cross Symbol
The imperfections of the burlap cross, its rough texture and unrefined fabric, the interweaving of threads, the uniqueness of each strand, are elements that are present within the covenant group. The people in the groups are imperfect, unpolished, interrelated with each other, yet still unique beings.

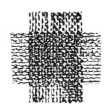

The shape that this collection of imperfect threads creates is the cross, symbolizing for all Christians the resurrection and presence of Christ our Savior. A covenant group is something akin to this burlap cross. It unites common, ordinary people and sends them out again in all directions to be in the world.

Creating Rituals for Your Group
One way to enrich this time is to create rituals or routines for the group that give the sharing and prayer time a special rhythm. For the *Esther* study, choose from the rituals that follow.

Setting the Table: Many times in this story the characters gather around a feasting table. You may choose to set a table each week with items that remain on the table or items that are surprises each week. Here are some ways you could set your table:

❑ Light candles, one for each participant, as each person arrives. You can then light the candles for those absent and remember them in prayer. You may develop a ritual unique to your group. For example, as you extinguish your candles each week, read a scripture or a prayer together.

❑ Take turns bringing in a loaf of bread for the table. The bread could be a different kind each time, reflecting the nature of the part of Esther you are reading (for example hard bread when the action is hard or celebration breads when the meal is a party). Share the bread at the end or beginning of each session.

❑ Invite people to bring in news clippings from the week that portray both violence and hope. Place the clippings on the table. People could then share how the act of violence or hope affects their faith this week. Esther is a book where violence and despair commingle with hope, so it is important to see both movements in our lives.

❑ Place an open hymnal or Bible on the table, and open it to a song or scripture that gives you hope. People could take turns doing this, or you could assign the task to one person for the entire ten weeks. Use the particular scripture and/or hymn in your worship together.

Sharing a Meal of Hope: Another way to create ritual around Esther's story is to make meals of hope together. You can do this as part of your service response. For example:

❑ Make sandwiches each week for a local shelter/feeding program.

❑ Bring a can of food each week for a local food program. Also encourage your congregation to get involved in a ten-week food collection.

❑ Sponsor a fellowship meal around a topic of interest for your congregation. Or perform a play for them (Creative Drama Services has some great ones). You could also host a meal for people who have been visiting your congregation or are new to your church.

❑ Plan potlucks once a week or on special nights. Some groups like to have meals together. For this meal-oriented story, eating together would be a great personal application!

Rituals of Prayer: While God and prayer are not specifically mentioned in the book of Esther, we know that community is molded by how we pray or don't pray together. A ritual of prayer for your group might involve these ideas:

❑ On a slip of paper, write about an aspect of your life in which you need courage in the coming week. Exchange slips with another person in your group, with the promise to pray once a day for that courage to come as a gift.

❑ Your group could covenant together to pray in unison wherever you are each day at a particular time (for example, at noon). Use a phrase from scripture or a prayer of one or several sentences that you write for this purpose. During group time you could share how this practice of prayer is changing for you.

❑ Each week, share songs that give you courage. Either use tapes or sing around a piano/organ/guitar during your group time. If the song is of special significance to one member, put that person in the middle of your circle and sing it to him or her. See the hymns at the conclusion of this study.

❑ Because Esther is a book conveying a theme of courage, offer prayers of encouragement with the laying on of hands. This could become a closing ritual each week for your group.

❑ Choose a scripture of encouragement and place the name of each member in the text and read it back to them. Or exchange scriptures and promise to pray them for each other during the week. For example, Psalm 23 would be, "The Lord is the shepherd of Cathy, she shall not want," etc.

❑ Take a prayer walk around a school, hospital, church, or part of your community. During a prayer walk, stop along the way to say a prayer for the particular place. For instance, if you pray around your church, you might go to each room and pray for those who have used that space and will use it in the future. If you pray at a hospital, you can go to each floor and pray in the open areas for the patients and staff on that floor. You may choose to walk around a school, praying for those who attend there. A prayer walk is also meaningful in your neighborhood where you meet as a group. How does praying in a different space change your experience of prayer? Does it make a difference where you pray?

❑ Sing a prayer song each week. See the conclusion of this resource section.

Rituals of Action: Engage in a ministry of encouragement each week. For example:

❑ Write a letter of gratitude/thanksgiving to a church member each week, using stationery that you create with the covenant symbol or your church logo. Spend some group time telling about the ways you are encouraged by the faith and actions of the people to whom you have written.

❑ Become "underground" greeters for your congregation on Sunday mornings by making a "stranger hunters" pact with each other. In other words, group members agree that following worship they will actively seek out someone who is new or they do not know well. The "stranger hunters" will offer words of encouragement and welcome to those folks before getting involved in conversations with friends.

❏ Decide to spend ten weeks in active support of your pastor(s) by doing a weekly act of kindness for them, perhaps anonymously. Pastors need encouragement and kindness to continue in their effective witness.

❏ Write letters of encouragement each week to leaders, both within and outside the church. Remind the recipients that you are praying for them, and then pray as a group.

Prayers and Hymns for Courage

The risen, living Christ
Calls us by our name;
Comes to the loneliness within us;
Heals that which is wounded within us;
Comforts that which grieves within us;
Seeks for that which is lost within us;
Releases us from that which has dominion over us;
Cleanses us of that which does not belong to us;
Renews that which feels drained within us;
Awakens that which is asleep in us;
Names that which is still formless within us;
Empowers that which is newborn within us;
Consecrates and guides that which is strong within us;
Restores us to this world which needs us;
Reaches out in endless love to others through us.
Amen.

From *Prayer, Fear, and Our Powers*, by Flora S. Wuellner, copyright © 1989, Upper Room Books, Nashville. Used by permission of the publisher.

O eternal Trinity,
my sweet love!
You, light,
give us light.
You, wisdom,
give us wisdom.
You, supreme strength,
strengthen us.
Today, eternal God,
let our cloud be dissipated
so that we may perfectly know and follow your truth,
in truth,
with a free and simple heart.

—Catherine of Siena

Let nothing trouble you,
Let nothing scare you,
All is fleeting,
God alone is unchanging.
Patience
Everything obtains.
Who possesses God
Nothing wants.
God alone suffices.

—Teresa of Avila

Christian, let your burning light

1 Chris-tian, let your burn-ing light   shine on all with   lus-ter bright.
2 As   you jour-ney   here be-low,   shed   a ray wher - e'er you go.
3 That your light may   guide you through, bright-ly let   it   shine a-new.

Let your words and   deeds be pure.   All   for Christ you   must en - dure.
Find in   this your   pure de-light,   let your light shine   clear and bright.
Keep up   cour-age – nev-er   fail   till you're safe with - in   the vail.

Refrain

Chris - tian, let   your light   shine,   all   a - long   your   way.

You   may guide   a wan - d'rer   to   e - ter - nal   day.

You may save from   end-less night   if you let your   lamp burn bright.

Text and music: E. G. Coleman, 1898

Lord, speak to me

1	Lord,	speak	to	me,	that	I	may	speak	in
2	O	lead	me,	Lord,	that	I	may	lead	the
3	O	strength - en	me,	that	while	I	stand	firm
4	O	teach	me,	Lord,	that	I	may	teach	the
5	O	fill	me	with	thy	full - ness,	Lord,	un
6	O	use	me,	Lord,	use	ev - en	me,	just

1	liv - ing	ech - oes	of	thy	tone.	As	thou hast sought, so
2	wan - d'ring	and	the	wav - 'ring	feet.	O	feed	me, Lord, that
3	on	the	Rock, and	strong	in	thee,	I	may stretch out	a
4	pre - cious things thou	dost	im - part,	and	wing	my words, that
5	til	my	ver - y	heart	o'er - flow	in	kin - dling thought and
6	as	thou	wilt, and	when	and where, un -	til	thy	bless - ed

1	let	me	seek	thine	err - ing	chil - dren	lost	and	lone.
2	I	may	feed	thy	hun - g'ring	ones	with	man - na	sweet.
3	lov - ing	hand	to	wres - tlers	with	the	trou - bled	sea.
4	they	may	reach	the	hid - den	depths	of	many	a	heart.
5	glow - ing	word,	thy	love	to	tell,	thy	praise	to	show.
6	face	I	see,	thy	rest,	thy	joy,	thy	glo - ry	share.

Text: Frances R. Havergal, 1872
Music: Robert Schumann, 1872, adapt.

Gracious Spirit, dwell with me

1 Gra - cious Spir - it, dwell with me: I my - self would
2 Truth - ful Spir - it, dwell with me: I my - self would
3 Si - lent Spir - it, dwell with me: I my - self would
4 Might - y Spir - it, dwell with me: I my - self would
5 Ho - ly Spir - it, dwell with me: I my - self would

1 gra - cious be, and, with words that help and heal,
2 truth - ful be, and, with wis - dom kind and clear,
3 qui - et be, qui - et as the grow - ing blade,
4 might - y be, might - y so as to pre - vail
5 ho - ly be, break from sin and choose the good,

1 would thy life in mine re - veal, and, with ac - tions
2 let thy life in mine ap - pear, and, with ac - tions
3 which through earth its way has made, si - lent - ly, like
4 where un - aid - ed I must fail, ev - er, by a
5 cher - ish what my Sav - ior would, and what - ev - er

1 bold and meek, would for Christ my Sav - ior speak.
2 lov - ing - ly, speak my Lord's sin - cer - i - ty.
3 morn - ing light, put - ting mists and chills to flight.
4 might - y hope, press - ing on and bear - ing up.
5 I can be give to him who gave me thee.

Text: Thomas T. Lynch, 1855, alt.
Music: Richard Redhead, 1853

Awake, my soul

1 A - wake, my soul, stretch ev - 'ry nerve, and press with vig - or
2 A cloud of wit - ness - es a - round holds thee in full sur -
3 'Tis God's all - an - i - mat - ing voice that calls thee from on
4 that prize, with peer - less glo - ries bright which shall new lus - ter
5 Bless'd Sav - ior, in - tro - duced by thee have I my race be -

1 on! A heav'n - ly race de - mands thy zeal, and
2 vey. For - get the steps al - read - y trod, and
3 high. 'Tis his own hand pre - sents the prize to
4 boast, when vic - tors' wreaths and mon - archs' gems shall
5 gun, and crowned with vic - t'ry at thy feet I'll

1 an im - mor - tal crown, and an im - mor - tal crown.
2 on - ward urge thy way, and on - ward urge thy way.
3 thine as - pir - ing eye, to thine as - pir - ing eye;
4 blend in com - mon dust, shall blend in com - mon dust.
5 lay my hon - ors down, I'll lay my hon - ors down.

Text: Philip Doddridge, 1755
Music: George Frederick Handel, 1728

Other Covenant Bible Studies

1 Corinthians: The Community Struggles (Inhauser)	$5.95
Abundant Living: Wellness from a Biblical Perspective	
(Rosenberger)	$4.95
Biblical Imagery for God (Bucher)	$5.95
Covenant People (Heckman/Gibble)	$5.95
Ephesians: Reconciled in Christ (Ritchey Martin)	$5.95
The Gospel of Mark (Ramirez)	$5.95
In the Beginning (Kuroiwa)	$5.95
James: Faith in Action (Young)	$5.95
Jonah: God's Global Reach (Bowser)	$4.95
The Life of David (Fourman)	$4.95
The Lord's Prayer (Rosenberger)	$4.95
Love and Justice (O'Diam)	$4.95
Many Cultures, One in Christ (Garber)	$5.95
Mystery and Glory in John's Gospel (Fry)	$5.95
Paul's Prison Letters (Bynum)	$5.95
Presence and Power (Dell)	$4.95
Psalms (Bowman)	$4.95
Real Families: From Patriarchs to Prime Time (Dubble)	$5.95
Revelation: Hope for the World in Troubled Times (Lowery)	$5.95
Sermon on the Mount (Bowman)	$4.95
A Spirituality of Compassion: Studies in Luke	
(Finney/Martin)	$5.95
Wisdom (Bowman)	$5.95

To place an order, call Brethren Press toll-free Monday through Friday, 8 a.m. to 4 p.m., at **800-441-3712** or fax an order to **800-667-8188** twenty-four hours a day. Shipping and handling will be added to each order. For a full description of each title, ask for a free catalog of these and other Brethren Press titles.

Visa and MasterCard accepted. Prices subject to change.

Brethren Press ● *faithQuest* ● 1451 Dundee Ave., Elgin, IL 60120-1694
800-441-3712 (orders) ● 800-667-8188